Cooking on the Run

A

NEW YORK FIREHOUSE C·O·O·K·B·O·O·K

JAMES J. POWELL

QUINLAN PRESS
Boston

Copyright © 1988
by James J. Powell

All rights reserved. No part of this publication may be reproduced or transmitted in any form or by any means, electronic or mechanical, including photocopy, recording, or any information storage and retrieval system, without the written permission of the publisher.

Published by Quinlan Press
131 Beverly Street, Boston, MA 02114

Printed in the United States of America, 1988.

Cover design by Lawrence Curcio.

Cover photo by Warren Fuchs.

All inside photographs courtesy of the F.D.N.Y. Forensic Unit.

Library of Congress Cataloging-in-Publication Data

Powell, James J., 1942-
  Cooking on the run.

  Includes index.
  1. Cookery, American. 2. New York (N.Y.). Fire Dept. I. Title.
TX715.P877   1987   641.5   87-43035
ISBN 0-933341-98-9 (pbk.)

This book is dedicated to those who love firefighters—those who fear that telephone call in the middle of a tour that begins "Honey, I'm all right, but...."; those who refuse to imagine anything worse than that terrible moment. It is to them, who do so much to make life so beautiful for firefighters, to whom I dedicate this work.

Thank you!

James J. Powell is a 1964 graduate of St. John's University. From 1968 to the present, he has been with the New York City Fire Department and has been decorated twice for bravery. From 1975 to 1981 he was a delegate to the Uniform Firefighters Association Union, and he was promoted to lieutenant in the fall of 1981.

Contents

Cooking Notes	vii
Introduction	ix
The Egg	1
Soups, Salads 'n' Stuff	9
Pasta	27
Beef, Pork and Lamb	43
Chicken	77
Seafood	87
Vegetables	101
Desserts	119
Index	127

Cooking Notes

The use of spirits in these recipes is strictly optional. I would ask, however, that you try the recipes as they are, at least for the first time. They have been carefully developed, and maximum flavor can only be achieved by following each recipe step by step. In the firehouse, Holland House brand cooking wines are used, but at home I use Carlo Rossi wines. The former are excellent, but the latter are more economical without sacrificing quality.

In regard to cooking spaghetti sauce, probably the most often overlooked step is the failure to skim the excess fat off the top of the sauce while it is cooking. The importance of this step can not be overemphasized, for reasons both of health and taste. Also, when cooking onions and garlic, do not add the garlic until the onions are soft. The idea is to brown the onions but only thoroughly heat the garlic. When garlic is browned, it becomes bitter.

Ideally, you should prepare soup a day ahead. This allows you to easily skim any congealed fat off the top before reheating, and it also allows the flavor of the soup to mature.

Introduction

Welcome to a unique and little-known part of your neighborhood—your firehouse! Firefighters around the world share a common bond which goes beyond racing to someone's call for help and placing themselves between you and danger: firehouse cooking, where the golden threads of brotherhood begin.

Try to picture a bunch of firefighter-types finishing up a roll call at the start of a fifteen-hour night tour. As they start checking out the apparatus and their firefighting equipment, the banter begins:

"You cookin' dinner tonight, Joe?"

"I cooked it last night, Murphy!"

"So what! Are you cookin' tonight or what?"

"Well, I'll cook, but I'll be damned if I'm goin' to the store!"

"All right, Mr. Macho, I'll go. How about spaghetti and meatballs?"

"Too late. How 'bout meatloaf?"

"You made that last night! Can't you cook anything else?"

"Okay, okay. How 'bout chili on cornbread?"

"That's fine with me, but don't make it so hot—last time you melted the fillings outta my head!"

"Hey, if you guys keep pussy-footin' around, the stores will all be closed—let's get a move on!"

And so it goes, in probably every firehouse around the world.

In some firehouses, competition for the role of cook is fierce. It's not uncommon for someone to show up an hour or more before the start of a night tour, just to get a jump on the next guy. A wise fire captain once set a rule that kept this rivalry on friendly terms for the members of his Harlem firehouse: "The first one to turn on all the burners on the stove will be the cook that night."

Why the race to be the night's cook? Anyone who has ever enjoyed watching others appreciate a meal he or she has prepared can imagine the challenge and the delight of firehouse cooking. Facing anywhere from five to fifteen outspoken food critics from almost every cultural background imaginable calls for nerves of steel, talent, a thick skin, and some darn good recipes.

During meal preparation, the cook often takes on the air of a master sergeant. He delegates responsibility—who's going to the store, who's going to peel the onions—and pulls the group together in one of the most pleasant traditions around. His reward is usually escape from the clean-up detail, but the meal better be good or he'll never hear the end of it.

Since the Big Apple has been the principle point of entry for almost every ethnic group coming to the United States, the firehouses in New York City have been particularly blessed. Each wave of immigrants has bequeathed a veritable smorgasbord of international recipes, and some of the best of those are offered here.

Ever since our time in the cave, few things have brought more people together faster than the mutual preparation and enjoyment of a beautiful meal. Nowhere is this more evident than in the firehouse, and what works in the firehouse will work for any couple or family. With the help of a freezer, one cooking session can provide two, three or four meals.

So come learn a little more about the firefighter's lifestyle the easy way, through the recipes of the firehouse cook — the most loved and the most abused member of any firehouse.

THE EGG

The egg may quite possibly be best loved in France. French recipes abound with pure and simple delight in the egg. Americans seem to abide the egg, but the joy doesn't seem to be in us. In FDNY firehouses, however, there seems to be a greater link to the French than in many parts of the country. First, we can enjoy the Statue of Liberty daily—a beautiful gift from the French people. Second, virtually every piece of FDNY apparatus carries a "scaling ladder." This unique lifesaving device, invented by the French, allows firefighters to climb the faces of buildings to reach victims trapped beyond the reach of "conventional" ladders. This was dramatically demonstrated recently at the General Post Office fire in Manhattan. So it may be more understandable for others to accept that members of the FDNY do eat quiche and do share many things with the French—including their love of the egg!

The Egg

Quiche a la New York

Be bold. Be brave. Or be square. Forty-four million Frenchmen can't be wrong. This is perfect served with Wall Street Spinach Salad and a well-chilled bottle of champagne.

4 eggs
2 c. heavy cream
½ tsp. salt
dash cayenne pepper
1 c. cubed ham
1 9-inch pie crust, unbaked and well-chilled
2 tbs. butter or margarine, melted
1 c. cubed Swiss cheese
½ lb. fresh mushrooms, cleaned and halved
6 bacon slices, cooked and crumbled

Preheat over to 425 degrees.

Mix eggs, heavy cream, salt and cayenne pepper in a blender at lowest setting for about one minute. Brush pie crust with butter or margarine. Sprinkle ham and Swiss cheese evenly in pie crust. Pour egg mixture over all. Bake for 20 minutes. Slide out of oven and sprinkle with mushrooms and crumbled bacon. Lower oven heat to 300 degrees and bake quiche for 35 minutes.

Yields: Four to six servings.

The Egg

The Egg

Must-go Omelette

The joy of this recipe is found in its combination of flavors and implementation of the old Puritan ethic: waste not, want not!

8 lg. eggs
¼ c. evaporated milk
2 tbs. mayonnaise
1 tsp. Worcestershire sauce
½ c. mashed potatoes
2 oz. cheddar, Swiss or American cheese, diced
2 tbs. water
salt and pepper to taste
2 tbs. butter or margarine
2 slices Genoa salami, diced
½ c. cubed ham, beef or pork
4 scallions, peeled and diced

In a blender combine eggs, milk, mayonnaise, Worcestershire sauce, mashed potatoes, cheese, water and salt and pepper to taste. Blend at medium setting until smooth.

In a large skillet, melt butter or margarine. Add salami, diced meat and scallions. Sauté until meat is heated through and scallions are soft. Pour egg mixture over sautéed meat. When slightly set, fold in half. Or simply cook like scrambled eggs.

For a delicious sandwich, toast up some English muffins and put a slice of tomato, a piece of lettuce and a ladle of eggs between two halves.

Yields: Four to six servings.

The Egg

Shirred Eggs with Chicken Livers

Been cutting back on the old cholesterol lately and still missing those delicious eggs? Why not try a special egg delight for dinner once or twice a month? This recipe is very versatile; you can substitute beef, pork, or even lamb for the chicken livers. It's fast—and it's easy. This recipe is nicely accompanied by Glorious Rockaway Cole Slaw or Wall Street Spinach Salad.

6 lg. eggs
½ pt. heavy cream
⅛ tsp. salt
dash black pepper
4 tbs. butter or margarine
½ lb. chicken livers
½ tsp. onion flakes

Separate eggs, carefully preserving yolks intact. In a blender, combine egg whites, cream, salt and pepper; blend at lowest setting until frothy, about 20 seconds.

Melt butter or margarine in a saucepan. Add chicken livers and onion flakes; sauté for about five minutes and drain. Pour cream mixture and chicken livers into a baking pan sprayed with a non-stick spray coating. Bake at 350 degrees until egg whites are firm, about 15 minutes.

Slide baking pan out of oven and carefully top with the egg yolks. Do not break the yolks. Return pan to oven for 2 minutes.

Yields: Three to four servings.

The Egg

Firehouse Eggs

This recipe has been around for almost fifty years. Some believe it was made famous in a movie about the Gas House Gang, but this recipe seems a bit removed from the type you might expect from such a group. In any event, I've enjoyed it in the firehouse and feel that this is a much more enticing title. I know you'll enjoy it no matter what you call it.

2 slices bread per person (I prefer Arnold's white)
½ c. butter or margarine, melted
2 lg. eggs per person

Preheat the griddle. Gently cut a hole about the size of a quarter in the center of each slice of bread. With pastry brush, generously coat both sides of each slice with melted butter or margarine.

Over medium heat, brown each slice of bread on one side. After each slice of bread is turned, break an egg into the center; the yolk should be directly over the hole. After one minute, turn carefully. Try not to break the yolks. Cook for another 30 seconds.

You can also coat one slice of tomato per egg with melted butter and grill while grilling eggs. Serve one slice on each egg.

The Egg

Three-bi Eggs

After a long hard night, the fireman who stands the three-to-six-a.m. watch can often find his stomach a little out of sorts. The following recipe helps him—as well as anyone else—get started on an "out of sorts" morning.

2 eggs
½ c. milk
⅛ tsp. salt
dash black pepper
1 tbs. butter or margarine

Combine eggs, milk, salt and pepper in a blender. Blend at a medium setting until frothy, about 15 seconds.

Melt butter or margarine in a small saucepan and add the egg mixture. Cook over medium heat until sauce is bubbling and eggs have solidified, about three minutes.

Yields: One serving.

Soups, Salads 'n' Stuff

A couple of firehouse adages apply to this section of recipes.

First, "No fire is the same" shows the firefighter's adaptability to the unique, as well as his quest to avoid the mundane.

Second, "You're only as good as your last fire" demonstrates the vulnerability each firefighter shares with his Brothers. Firefighters must *know* how good the person alongside them—male or female—really is, because if things "heat up" their lives will be in the hands of that person.

When you find a person who will bring the untried and different recipes into the firehouse, you have found a person of unique courage, self-assurance and pride. In other words, you've found a person you can depend on.

Soups, Salads 'n' Stuff

Belmont Barley Soup

No one can prepare this meal without feeling the flavor of our American roots, even though certain modern conveniences are employed. The aroma of beef, barley and spices only hints at the wonderful flavor.

2 oz. Burgundy wine
1 tbs. Worcestershire sauce
½ tsp. garlic powder
½ tsp. dry mustard
½ tsp. paprika
½ tsp. sage
1½ to 2 lbs. flank steak
3 tbs. vegetable oil
1 envelope of onion soup mix
2 quarts water
4 beef bouillon cubes
¾ c. barley
3 medium carrots, peeled and diced
3 medium celery stalks, diced
1 medium onion, peeled and diced
2 tbs. chopped parsley

Combine wine and Worcestershire sauce with the garlic powder, dry mustard, paprika and sage. When thoroughly mixed, brush over both sides of the flank steak. Preserve any remaining wine mixture. Heat the oil in a Dutch oven and brown the meat on both sides. Turn off the heat, remove the meat and slice it into thin julienne-like strips.

Return the julienned beef to the Dutch oven and sprinkle the envelope of onion soup mix over the meat and add any leftover wine mixture. Simmer for approximately 30 minutes, stirring occasionally. Add up to 2 oz. each of additional water and wine if necessary. Add the 2 quarts of water and bouillon cubes to the Dutch oven and bring to a boil; then lower the

Soups, Salads 'n' Stuff

heat and simmer for approximately 1 hour. Add the barley, diced carrots, celery and onion to the soup and simmer for an additional hour. Stir in the chopped parsley and simmer for 5 to 6 minutes.

Serve piping hot!

Yields: Six to eight servings.

Soups, Salads 'n' Stuff

JFK Pea Soup

Even when the fog is as thick as pea soup, JFK Airport gets the job done. So does this recipe. When the cool weather approaches, nothing will draw them into the kitchen faster than this aroma.

2 bacon strips, diced
2 onions, peeled and diced
1 lg. garlic clove, peeled and crushed
2 tbs. chopped fresh parsley
⅛ tsp. dill weed
⅛ tsp. crushed mint leaves
⅛ tsp. sage
⅛ tsp. thyme
½ tsp. salt
1 tsp. soy sauce
¼ c. Rhine wine
3 beef bouillon cubes
1 ham bone
1 16-oz. pkg. green split peas
1 lg. carrot, peeled and grated
1 bay leaf
1 tsp. celery salt
3 peppercorns
1 6-oz. pkg. split pea mix seasoning (I use Manischewitz)
3 lg. potatoes, peeled and diced
1 tbs. butter
1 c. half 'n' half cream

Place bacon in an eight-quart pot over low heat. Add onions and sauté until soft, 3 to 5 minutes. Stir in garlic, parsley, dill, mint, sage, thyme and salt. Raise heat to medium, and stir-fry for another 3 to 5 minutes. Add soy sauce, Rhine wine, bouillon cubes and ham bone; mix everything well. Add water and washed split peas and bring mixture to a boil. Mix

Soups, Salads 'n' Stuff

in carrot, bay leaf, celery salt, peppercorns and package of seasoning.

When soup comes to a boil, lower heat and simmer, covered, for 2 hours, stirring every 20 minutes or so. Uncover and add diced potatoes; continue to simmer for 30 minutes. Stir in butter and half 'n' half. Serve immediately, preferably with a loaf of bakery-fresh pumpernickel or onion-rye bread.

Yields: Eight to ten servings.

Soups, Salads 'n' Stuff

Aqueduct Chicken Escarole Soup

Aqueduct Racetrack, located in the borough of Queens, is known internationally. During the winter months very little goes on except for the weekend Flea Markets. This recipe was inspired after spending a full day outside on the winter's coldest day. Few meals will warm your heart *and everything else*, the way this recipe will.

1 sm. head/bunch of escarole
2 quarts College Inn chicken broth
2 chicken cutlets
2 oz. cold Rhine wine
1 tbs. flour
4 eggs
¼ tsp. salt
Dash of cayenne pepper
½ c. grated Parmesan cheese

To prepare: Separate the escarole into individual leaves, wash thoroughly and then soak in cold water until you are ready for them. In an 8-quart soup pot, bring chicken broth to a boil. Cut the chicken cutlets into thin julienne-like strips. In a mixing bowl, slowly mix the wine with the flour. After they are thoroughly combined, beat in the eggs, salt and cayenne pepper. Mix thoroughly. Slowly add 1 ladle of broth to the mixture, and combine thoroughly.

To cook: When the chicken broth comes to a boil, add the julienned chicken cutlets and the escarole leaves. Lower heat to simmer, and continue cooking for about 20 minutes until the escarole leaves are tender. Add the egg/broth mixture to the soup. While the soup is simmering, sprinkle the Parmesan cheese over the top and continue to simmer for 3 to 5 minutes until the cheese becomes stringy.

Yields: Six to eight servings.

Soups, Salads 'n' Stuff

Bayside Blue Cheese Dressing

This dressing will make a blue-cheese devotee sigh with satisfaction.

6 oz. blue cheese, crumbled
1 sm. onion, peeled and diced
1 garlic clove, peeled and crushed
1 c. mayonnaise
¼ c. ketchup
¼ c. olive oil
¼ c. Rhine wine
2 tbs. apple vinegar
½ tsp. paprika
½ tsp. poppy seeds
½ tsp. salt
½ tsp. Dijon mustard
⅛ tsp. cayenne pepper

Blend all ingredients except blue cheese in a blender until smooth. Stir in crumbled blue cheese and mix thoroughly; refrigerate for 15 to 30 minutes.

This recipe makes the ideal amount of dressing for Parkslope Reuben Casserole.

Yields: Approximately 1 cup.

Central Park Summer Lunch Salad

Believe me when I tell you, this is what the picnic hampers in all those French Impressionist paintings held.

1 lb. bacon, cooked and crumbled
¼ lb. Swiss cheese, cubed
2 oz. cheddar cheese, cubed
¼ lb. ham, cubed
2 lg. celery stalks, chopped
½ lb. radishes, cleaned and halved
½ lb. fresh mushrooms, cleaned and halved
1 c. mayonnaise
¼ c. Rhine wine
2 tbs. onion flakes
1 tbs. Dijon mustard
1 tbs. lemon juice
1 tbs. chopped fresh parsley
¼ tsp. garlic powder
dash cayenne pepper
6 hard-boiled eggs, chopped
2 lg. lettuce leaves per plate
4 tomatoes, quartered

In a large salad bowl, combine bacon, cheeses, ham, celery, radishes and mushrooms.

In a blender at lowest setting, mix mayonnaise, wine, onion flakes, Dijon mustard, lemon juice, parsley, garlic powder and cayenne pepper for about 30 seconds. Add chopped eggs and blend at lowest setting for about 15 seconds.

Add dressing to salad and toss thoroughly. Place lettuce on plates, cover with salad and garnish with tomato wedges.

Soups, Salads 'n' Stuff

Mr. Macho's Antipasto

This relatively easy recipe deserves its name. It took something special to prepare it in the firehouse the first time. Peeling and slicing the onions was the easy part. Fielding the comments, questions and faces was what really took courage. If you have the courage, try this one. You are in for a truly unique delight.

3 lbs. Bermuda onions, peeled, sliced into rings and separated into individual rings
2 small cans anchovy fillets (chopped), oil included
1/4 tsp. red pepper flakes
1/8 tsp. basil
1/8 tsp. oregano

Place onion rings in a large bowl, add chopped anchovies with oil, sprinkle spices over the top. Mix everything thoroughly. Cover bowl with plastic wrap and refrigerate overnight. Ideally the antipasto should be mixed 3 or 4 times during this period. Remove from refrigerator about 1 hour before serving, uncover, mix again and allow the antipasto to settle.

Serve with a simple green salad and a loaf of fresh Italian semolina bread.

Yields: Four to six servings.

Soups, Salads 'n' Stuff

Unpretentious Cole Slaw

You can't deny that sometimes the quick and easy is the best — and nothing else will do.

1 sm. cabbage head, outer leaves removed
3 med. carrots
¾ c. mayonnaise
1 tbs. milk

Quarter cabbage head, then slice into thin strips. Using a scraper, slice carrots into thin strips. In a salad bowl, mix mayonnaise and milk. Add cabbage and carrot strips to salad bowl and toss.

Refrigerate slaw for 10 to 15 minutes prior to serving. Toss again and serve.

Yields: Six to eight servings.

Soups, Salads 'n' Stuff

Sunnyside Tuna Salad

This recipe was created by combining three mundane lunchtime fares and adding a little imagination. Take a little time—you'll be nicely rewarded for your effort.

½ lb. elbow macaroni, cooked in unsalted water
12 hard-boiled eggs, divided
2 cans white tuna in spring water, drained
1 c. mayonnaise
1 sm. onion, peeled and diced
1 med. carrot, peeled and diced
1 med. celery stalk, washed and diced
fresh spinach
4 lg. tomatoes, sliced

Place cooked macaroni in a large salad bowl. Shred four eggs into salad bowl; slice remaining eight in half and set aside. Mix in tuna, mayonnaise, onion, carrot and celery. Place in refrigerator to chill.

Wash spinach, cut off stems and arrange three or four large leaves on each plate. Place a generous ladle of tuna salad in middle of each spinach arrangement. Garnish with two slices of tomato and two hard-boiled egg halves.

Yields: Eight servings.

Soups, Salads 'n' Stuff

Glorious Rockaway Cole Slaw

It was quite a surprise to me when I heard a group of firefighters "negotiating" with another Brother to make his cole slaw for lunch! Cole slaw??? Well, it didn't take more than the initial taste for me to realize just how lucky I was to be in the right place at the right time. It has taken me years to replicate that glorious taste. I know that you'll enjoy it.

4 c. shredded raw green cabbage
2 c. shredded raw carrot
6 tbs. fresh lemon juice
2-3 oz. jars red pimientos, diced
4 tbs. fresh diced parsley
6 shallots, diced
1 tsp. salt
$^2/_3$ cup half 'n half cream
2 tbs. ketchup
3 tsp. Dijon mustard
4 tsp. apple cider vinegar
¼ tsp. nutmeg
¼ tsp. cayenne pepper
¼ tsp. paprika

Combine cabbage, carrots, lemon juice and toss. Add pimientos, parsley, shallots, and 1 tsp. salt.

Pour the remaining ingredients into a blender and blend for 2 to 3 minutes. Pour mixture over the slaw and toss.

Yields: Six to eight servings.

Soups, Salads 'n' Stuff

Wall Street Spinach Salad

In the late 1970s, a U.F.A. president led his union from City Hall to Wall Street. It didn't take the financial wizards long to hear our message. Whether it had any impact on our contract negotiations or not, only people more in the know than I can say. I had lunch in one of those upscale restaurants and came away with this, one of my all-time favorite salad recipes. I know you'll like it too.

1 lb. fresh spinach
½ lb. fresh mushrooms, cleaned and halved
1 lg. egg
⅓ c. Rhine wine
¼ c. lemon juice
¼ c. apple vinegar
2 tbs. soy sauce
3 tbs. bacon bits
¼ tsp. garlic powder
¼ tsp. onion powder
⅛ tsp. salt
⅛ tsp. cayenne pepper

Thoroughly wash spinach. Remove stems and tear leaves into bite-size pieces, place in a large bowl and put in freezer for about 5 minutes. Blend remaining ingredients, except mushrooms, in a blender until smooth.

Remove spinach from freezer, add mushrooms and egg mixture, toss thoroughly and serve immediately.

Yields: Four to six servings.

Soups, Salads 'n' Stuff

Go For It Garlic Bread

Almost fifteen years ago, I was preparing a spaghetti dinner in the firehouse and I found myself hesitating over the garlic bread. I mean, every cook makes garlic bread to one degree or another. The degree—of garlic—was, of course, my problem. When my friend Tom strolled into the kitchen and realized my dilemma, he said, "Don't be afraid—be yourself. Go for it!" Well, I did and the result is before you. One taste and you'll agree that you should "go for it" in everything you do.

1/3 c. Rhine wine
1 tsp. Parmesan cheese
1 tsp. chopped fresh parsley
1/8 tsp. Italian red pepper
1/8 tsp. basil
1/8 tsp. oregano
1 lg. loaf Italian bread
1/3 c. olive oil
6 lg. garlic cloves, peeled and crushed
1 sm. onion, peeled and diced
1/2 c. butter or margarine

In a measuring cup, mix wine, cheese, parsley, red pepper, basil and oregano. Slice bread lengthwise but not quite through.

In a saucepan, heat oil; add garlic, onion and butter or margarine. Cook over medium heat until butter melts, stirring occasionally. Add wine mixture and simmer for 5 minutes, again stirring occasionally.

Soups, Salads 'n' Stuff

Preheat toaster oven to 300 degrees. Ladle mixture generously over both sections of the bread's insides. Bake the bread open at 300 degrees for 5 minutes, or until the edges begin to brown. Remove from toaster oven, close the bread and slice.

Yields: Four to six servings.

Soups, Salads 'n' Stuff

Keep 'em Up Popcorn

3 qts. unsalted popcorn
¼ c. melted butter
½ can french fried onions
¼ tsp. cayenne pepper
¼ c. bacon bits
salt to taste

Preheat oven to 300 degrees.

Toss popped corn with melted butter. Stir in french fried onions, cayenne pepper and bacon bits. Sprinkle with salt. Place mixture on a baking sheet.

Heat in oven for a few minutes. Serve hot.

Soups, Salads 'n' Stuff

Paddy's Day Bread

¼ lb. butter
¾ c. sugar
2 extra large eggs
3 c. sifted flour
1 c. heavy cream
4 tsp. baking powder
1 tsp. salt
2 tbs. caraway seeds
4 oz. raisins

Preheat oven to 350 degrees.

Melt butter in a large saucepan, then remove from heat and allow to cool. Stir in sugar. Add eggs and beat thoroughly. Alternately, add ¼ of the flour and ¼ of the cream, mixing well after each addition until batter is completely formed. Add remaining ingredients and mix thoroughly into batter. (It will be a stiff mix.)

Place batter in a buttered bread pan and bake for 1 hour, or until a toothpick inserted in the middle comes out clean.

Yields: One loaf.

PASTA

Few imports fit the American culinary appetite better than pasta. Created in China, personalized in Italy, and adored in New York, pasta is one staple that lends itself to the full spectrum of culinary possibilities. Come and enjoy some of the favorites found in Big Apple firehouses.

Pasta

Elizabeth Street Spaghetti Sauce

Second, third or higher alarms always leave varied impressions on the firefighters who experience them. However, one common impression, perhaps the most common, is how all that hose stretched absolutely everywhere looks like spaghetti. So I ask you, with all our experience, who could make a better spaghetti sauce?

Meatballs and/or braciole, along with a green salad and a fresh loaf of Italian semolina bread, are great companions to this recipe.

½ c. Chianti wine
2 tbs. chopped fresh parsley
2 tsp. salt
2 tbs. grated Parmesan cheese
4 tbs. olive oil
1 lb. package pork neck bones
4 med. onions, peeled and chopped
4 med. garlic cloves, peeled and crushed
1 tsp. basil
1 tsp. oregano
⅛ tsp. Italian red pepper
1 6-oz. can tomato paste
1 28-oz. can crushed tomatoes
1 28-oz. can tomato puree
2 28-oz. cans water
½ lb. fresh mushrooms, washed and halved

In a measuring cup, combine wine, parsley, salt and Parmesan cheese. In a large pot, heat 2 tbs. oil. Add pork neck bones and onions; brown over medium heat until onions are golden. Stir in remaining oil with garlic, basil, oregano and pepper. Sauté until onions are clear, about three minutes. Add paste, crushed tomatoes, puree and water. Bring sauce to a boil, then stir in wine and herb mixture and mushrooms.

Pasta

Cover and simmer for about 2 hours, skimming excess fat from surface every 20 minutes or so—this is very important. (If you want meatballs with your sauce, this is where you should start the recipe for Italian Meatballs.)

Serve with pasta (I like Ronzoni Fusilli #115), Go For It Garlic Bread and a crisp green salad.

Yields: Eight to ten servings.

Pasta

Whitestone's Linguine with Clam Sauce

A number of years ago, after getting a break at an All Hands fire (that's a full first alarm assignment at work) one of the guys said, "Hey, Lieu, call the dispatcher and ask him to tell the relocated (covering) company not to mess with our clam sauce! No matter how long we're here." If you try this recipe you'll know how it can create such loyalty.

Some fresh Italian semolina bread and a green salad accentuate this meal perfectly.

¼ c. Rhine wine
¼ c. Parmesan cheese
1 tbs. chopped fresh parsley
1 tsp. lemon juice
⅛ tsp. basil
dash Italian red pepper
½ c. olive oil
1 lg. onion, peeled and diced
3 med. garlic cloves, peeled and crushed
2 tbs. butter or margarine
1 10 ½-oz. can minced clams
1 8-oz. bottle clam juice
1 lb. linguine

In a large measuring cup, combine wine, cheese, parsley, lemon juice, basil and pepper flakes. In a medium size saucepan, combine oil, onion, garlic and butter or margarine; sauté until onion is soft. Add the wine mixture, the juice from minced clams and the bottle of clam juice. Cover and simmer about 10 minutes. Add minced clams.

While clam sauce simmers, cook linguine according to package directions. Just before draining, add ½ c. pasta water to clam sauce and stir well.

Pasta

Place the drained linguine in a large serving bowl, top with clam sauce and serve immediately with plenty of freshly grated Parmesan cheese.

Yields: Four to six servings.

Pasta

Rosedale's Fettucine a la Franco

This recipe is ideal for those occasions when you need something special but don't have a great deal of time or energy. Of course, it's also great when you have both of those ingredients! This meal is beautifully accented by Go For It Garlic Bread and a fresh garden salad.

1 lb. fettucine
½ c. butter or margarine
1 egg
¼ c. dry white wine
½ pt. light cream
½ c. grated Parmesan cheese
2 tbs. chopped fresh parsley
dash cayenne pepper

Cook fettucine according to package directions. Drain in a colander.

In the now-empty pasta pot, melt butter and return fettucine; mix well. In a small bowl, beat egg. Add remaining ingredients and mix well.

Stir egg mixture over buttered fettucine and toss thoroughly. Serve piping hot with plenty of extra Romano cheese and freshly ground black pepper on the table.

Yields: Four to six servings.

Pasta

Bensonhurst Creamy Casserole

This recipe is as stable as the neighborhood it's named for—unpretentious, wholesome and unique. Wall Street Spinach Salad is a nice accompaniment to this recipe. You can also add a can of white tuna in water (drained) to the tomato mixture. It makes for an almost totally different taste, but it's just as delicious.

1 lb. elbow macaroni
2 c. crushed tomatoes
1 c. Velveeta cheese, cubed
1 c. milk
3 tbs. grated cheddar cheese

Preheat oven to 350 degrees.

Cook macaroni according to package directions; drain and return to pot. Add tomatoes, Velveeta and milk; mix thoroughly. Place mixture in a large ovenproof casserole dish, sprinkle with grated cheddar cheese and bake for 30 minutes.

Yields: Four to six servings.

Pasta

SoHo Italian Casserole

In Manhattan, SoHo is the area South of Houston Street that borders New York's Little Italy. This area is one of the strongholds of the Big Apple's Yuppies, and abounds with all of their finery. This recipe enhances the rich influence of this special locale with the finest Italian cuisine.

4 chicken breasts, cubed
1 egg, beaten
5 tbs. whole wheat flour
1 lb. rigatoni (I prefer Ronzoni #27)
6 tbs. butter or margarine
1 lg. onion, peeled and thinly sliced
dash Italian red pepper
3 garlic cloves, peeled and crushed
1 c. cubed ham
½ lb. fresh mushrooms
¼ c. Marsala (or, in a pinch, cream sherry)
1 c. half 'n' half
2 13¾-oz. cans chicken broth
¾ c. grated Romano cheese
⅛ tsp. salt

Dip cubed chicken in beaten egg, dredge with flour and set aside. Save any leftover flour and egg.

Prepare rigatoni according to package directions, but only boil for 8 minutes; drain and set aside. In a Dutch oven, melt butter or margarine and add onion and red pepper; sauté until onion is soft. Raise heat and add garlic, chicken, ham and mushrooms. Cook until meat is browned, about 6 minutes. Stir in Marsala, half 'n' half, chicken broth, any leftover flour or egg, half of Romano cheese and salt.

Bring to a boil and lower immediately. Simmer for 15 minutes, then stir in rigatoni and mix well. Top with remaining Romano cheese. Place Dutch oven in preheated 350 degree oven for 20 minutes.

Yields: Six to eight servings.

Pasta

Mott Street Pasta e Fagioli

In many ways a firehouse is a microcosm of the larger American society, for its members are drawn from almost every ethnic and cultural background. Consequently, when an "ethnic specialty" is prepared, the reactions from the diners can be quite varied. Let me share a little dialogue from some of the non-Italian Brothers when Pasta e Fagioli was served:
"*I never knew Pasta FA-ZOO-LEE was made with beans.*"
"*What kinda' beans are these, anyway?*"
"*They don't taste like any beans I ever met.*"
"*This is different ... but it's pretty good.*"
"*Yeah, I guess I could enjoy this once or twice a year.*"

Take it from me, you rarely get higher compliments when serving something new and different in the firehouse. I know that if you try this recipe, you'll enjoy a beautifully pleasant and yet different taste.

3 tbs. olive oil
1 med. onion, peeled and chopped
1 tsp. salt
½ tsp. basil
½ tsp. oregano
½ tsp. parsley
⅛ Italian red pepper
1 28-oz. can crushed tomatoes
2 lg. garlic cloves, peeled and crushed
1 20-oz. can kidney beans
1 lb. spaghetti

Pasta

Heat oil in a large saucepan. Add onion, salt, basil, oregano, parsley and red pepper; sauté until onion is soft. Add crushed tomatoes and garlic; simmer for 20 minutes. Stir in kidney beans with liquid and simmer for 15 minutes.

Cook spaghetti according to package directions. Drain and place in a large serving bowl. Pour sauce on top and mix well. Serve with grated Parmesan cheese.

Yields: Four to six servings.

Pasta

One-Two-Three Lasagna

Even on a busy night, you can make this delicious recipe.

8 c. Elizabeth Street Spaghetti Sauce
4 c. water
½ c. Chianti wine
2 lbs. ricotta cheese
1 lb. mozzarella, shredded
2 eggs
1 tsp. salt
½ c. Parmesan cheese
1 tbs. chopped fresh parsley
1 tsp. garlic powder
1 8-oz. can sliced mushrooms, drained
2 lbs. lasagna noodles

Preheat oven to 350 degrees.

Spray two baking pans with a non-stick spray coating. Mix 4 c. spaghetti sauce with water and wine. In a separate bowl, mix ricotta, shredded mozzarella, eggs, salt, Parmesan cheese, parsley and garlic powder.

Cover bottom of both baking pans with a layer of diluted sauce mixture. Place one layer of uncooked noodles over sauce. Spread ricotta mixture over noodles. Sprinkle mushrooms over ricotta. Place a generous ladle of sauce over all. Repeat this process until all ingredients are used, ending with a layer of sauce.

Cover baking pans with aluminum foil and bake for 45 minutes. Remove foil and bake 15 minutes longer. Serve with remaining 4 c. undiluted spaghetti sauce.

Yields: Eight to ten servings.

Pasta

Linguini de L'Ortello

This delicious recipe used to go by such unsavory titles as "Muddy Worms" in the firehouse. I think you'll agree that anything that tastes so fantastic deserves a more exalted name.

1 lb. linguini
3 tbs. olive oil
1 sm. onion, chopped
4 oz. anchovies, chopped
2 lg. cloves of garlic, crushed
8 oz. pitted black Italian olives, chopped
1 tsp. capers, chopped
2 fresh plum tomatoes, peeled and sliced into rings
2 oz. red wine
1 tsp. parsley flakes

Cook the linguini according to package directions.

Heat olive oil in a frying pan, and sauté onions until translucent. Add anchovies, garlic, olives, capers, tomato rings and cook for 3 minutes, stirring as needed. Lower heat to simmer, add wine and parsley, mix well and continue cooking for 4 to 5 minutes. When linguini is cooked and drained, add approximately half the sauce and mix well, then add remaining sauce on top.

A simple green salad and a fresh loaf of Italian semolina bread set off this dish perfectly.

Yields: Four to six servings.

Pasta

Spring Street Pasta

It takes more than your ordinary meat and potatoes to keep a firefighter's energy level up. This Pasta Primavera recipe, first enjoyed on Spring Street a number of years ago, is just the ticket. I know you'll enjoy this change of pace year round.

1 chicken bouillon cube, dissolved in 6 oz. boiling water
1 c. half 'n' half
¼ c. Rhine wine
½ tsp. fresh chopped parsley
½ tsp. oregano
1 tsp. salt
pinch Italian red pepper
¼ c. butter or margarine
6 lg. onions, peeled and chopped
3 lg. garlic cloves, peeled and crushed
1 med. carrot, peeled and thinly sliced
1 red bell pepper, cored and thinly sliced
½ lb. fresh mushrooms, washed and halved
1 box frozen broccoli or cauliflower
1 box frozen zucchini
4 lg. fresh tomatoes, quartered
¾ c. grated Parmesan cheese
1 lb. linguini

Combine bouillon, half 'n' half, wine, parsley, oregano, salt and red pepper.

In a large skillet, melt butter or margarine and add onion, sautéing until soft. Stir in garlic and all vegetables, except for tomatoes. Stir-fry until heated through, about 6 minutes. Pour in cream mixture and raise heat for about 5 minutes but do not boil. Add tomatoes and cook for about 2 minutes, or until they are heated. Turn off heat and cover skillet.

Pasta

Prepare linguini according to package directions. Drain and place in a large serving bowl. Top with sauce and Parmesan cheese, tossing thoroughly to coat. Serve piping hot with fresh Italian bread and an ice cold glass of rosé wine.

Yields: Six to eight servings.

Poppied Noodles

1 lb. egg noodles
¼ c. butter or margarine
3 tbs. poppy seeds
¼ tsp. salt

Cook egg noodles *al dente*. Drain, return to pot and add butter or margarine, poppy seeds and salt, stirring until butter melts.

BEEF, PORK AND LAMB

The "meat 'n' potatoes" firefighter—and in fact, most firefighters—tends just to want to get to the meal quickly, without fuss, without muss, and without any variation from the way it tasted the last time and the time before that and the time....

The recipes in this section take the basic items on such a person's menu and prepares them in ways that will quickly bring new vistas of taste and sophistication to palates long denied the joys of gourmet dining.

Beef, Pork and Lamb

Yorktown's Roast Beef

In this day of sleek, modern apparatus, it is nice to know that not only do the special traditions that earned the FDNY the title "the Bravest" continue—so also do the best recipes. Yorktown's Roast Beef is one such recipe. Named for an elegant section in the borough of Manhattan, this is an elegant firehouse favorite.

This roast should be served with Finger-lickin' Mashed Potatoes and Castelton Corners Creamed Carrots and Cauliflower.

1 4-lb. beef roast
meat tenderizer
2 tbs. whole wheat flour
¼ c. burgundy wine
2 tbs. Dijon mustard
1 tsp. onion powder
1 tsp. Worcestershire sauce
½ tsp. garlic powder
¼ tsp. paprika
¼ tsp. salt
pinch cayenne pepper
4 bacon strips, uncooked

Preheat oven to 325 degrees.

Spray a roasting pan with non-stick spray coating, then coat with 1 tbs. flour.

Pierce roast thoroughly with a fork and sprinkle with meat tenderizer. Place in a large dish. In a mixing cup, combine wine, mustard, 1 tbs. flour, onion powder, Worcestershire sauce, garlic powder, paprika, salt and cayenne pepper; mix thoroughly. Coat roast with wine and herb mixture, and allow it to stand for 5 minutes or so.

Beef, Pork and Lamb

Remove roast to the prepared roasting pan. Scoop up residual coating and ladle on top of roast. Place bacon strips evenly across top. Bake 20 minutes per pound for rare, 25 minutes per pound for medium, 30 minutes per pound for well done.

Yields: Six to eight servings.

Beef, Pork and Lamb

Glendale Pot Roast

This recipe, named for an old German neighborhood in the borough of Queens, is no longer prepared in NYC firehouses. The Department's Rules and Regulations always discouraged the use of "spirits" in the firehouse—even for cooking—but about fifteen years ago, the R&R's were given much sharper teeth. All Unit Circular 202 brought a penalty of ten days pay for a single can of beer. So, as you can see, this old favorite could be quite expensive—unless it is prepared at home and then, after the alcohol has cooked away, brought in as a special dinner.

A loaf of onion-rye bread and a bottle of a hearty red table wine set this meal off perfectly.

3 garlic cloves, peeled and crushed
½ tsp. salt
⅓ c. Chianti
½ tsp. horseradish
¼ tsp. sage
1 c. boiling water
2 beef bouillon cubes
1 bay leaf
1 tbs. fresh chopped parsley
½ tsp. thyme
6 white peppercorns
1 6-lb. rump roast
¼ c. butter or margarine
2 cans beer
6 sm. onions, peeled
6 med. potatoes, peeled and halved
6 med. carrots, peeled and quartered

Beef, Pork and Lamb

Mix garlic, salt, Chianti, horseradish and sage together to form a paste. In boiling water, dissolve bouillon cubes, then add bay leaf, parsley, thyme and peppercorns.

Pierce roast all over with a fork. Rub garlic paste thoroughly into meat. In a Dutch oven, melt butter or margarine; add roast and brown meat. Pour in bouillon mixture and 1 can of beer. Bring mixture to a boil, then lower heat and simmer, covered, for 1½ hours.

Remove lid from Dutch oven and turn meat. Pour in remaining can of beer and bring to a boil. Add onions, potatoes and carrots; lower heat to simmer. Cover and simmer for another hour or so, or until vegetables are done.

Remove roast from Dutch oven and let stand for 10 minutes before slicing. Discard bay leaf from gravy. Serve with Poppied Noodles.

Yields: Eight to ten servings.

Beef, Pork and Lamb

Washington Square Stroganoff

Washington Square is located at the foot of the Big Apple's main street: 5th Avenue. It is steeped in New York history and affluence. The Square is also bounded by Greenwich Village, the traditional Bohemian neighborhood of New York. These two diverse yet sympathetic influences blend together to give New York a special flavor. What better name to hint at the subtleties of a New York Stroganoff.

A large bowl of steamed and buttered fresh string beans set this dish off nicely. I also highly recommend a loaf of bakery-fresh pumpernickel on the side.

½ c. water
¼ c. burgundy wine
1 beef bouillon cube
¼ tsp. salt
¼ tsp. paprika
⅛ tsp. cayenne pepper
⅛ tsp. Dijon mustard
1 tbs. soy sauce
2 c. plain yogurt
4 tbs. whole wheat flour
2 bacon strips, cooked and crumbled
2 lbs. london broil, cubed
1 lb. lean ground beef
1 lg. onion, peeled and thinly sliced
½ lb. fresh mushrooms, washed and halved
3 garlic cloves, peeled and crushed
1 10½-oz. can condensed mushroom soup
1 lb. egg noodles

In a large measuring cup, combine water, wine, bouillon cube, salt, paprika, cayenne pepper, mustard and soy sauce. In a salad bowl, combine the yogurt, flour and crumbled bacon; mix well.

Beef, Pork and Lamb

In a Dutch oven, brown steak and ground beef. Drain off excess fat. Add onion, mushrooms and garlic to the meat; sauté until onion is soft. Stir in condensed soup and wine and herb mixture. Bring to a boil, cover and simmer for 20 minutes.

Cook egg noodles according to package directions. Uncover Dutch oven and blend in yogurt mixture; heat through, about 10 minutes. Serve the stroganoff on individual plates of egg noodles.

Yields: Six servings.

Beef, Pork and Lamb

Staten Island Beef Stew

The borough of Staten Island has experienced a renaissance since the opening of the Verrazzano Narrows Bridge. While many families have found new homes in this rapidly expanding borough, many pre-bridge "pioneers" miss the old neighborhood. When the only access from the other four boroughs was by ferry, Islanders enjoyed an air of rugged individualism. By one account, they were part of Broadway, Wall Street and Lincoln Center. Yet prior to the bridge, these Islanders could easily enjoy the classic beauty of American rural life. It shouldn't be difficult to appreciate why pre-bridgers were not anxious to share the secrets of their home life with the rest of the metropolis. This pre-bridge recipe blends the classic beauty of rural America with the sophisticated flavors of a modern metropolis. But out of respect to Staten Island's pre-bridge pioneers, let's keep it our little secret.

¼ c. vegetable oil
1 lb. pork neck bones
½ c. whole wheat flour
2 tsp. paprika
¼ tsp. thyme
¼ tsp. sage
⅛ tsp. cayenne pepper
3 lbs. round steak, cut into bite-size cubes
3 c. water
1 tsp. Worcestershire sauce
1 beef bouillon cube
1 chicken bouillon cube
1 envelope dry onion soup mix
1 c. burgundy wine
1 bay leaf
1 tbs. fresh chopped parsley
1 tbs. lemon juice
1 tsp. salt

Beef, Pork and Lamb

1 tsp. horseradish
1 tsp. Pickapeppa sauce (or steak sauce of your choice)
1 lg. yellow onion, peeled and diced
2 garlic cloves, peeled and crushed
½ c. sliced pepperoni
1 15-oz. can straw mushrooms
12 small white onions, peeled, or 6 shallots, peeled and sliced
4 lg. potatoes, peeled and quartered
4 lg. carrots, peeled and quartered

In a large Dutch oven, heat half of the oil. Add pork neck bones and brown; set aside. In a brown lunchbag, combine flour, paprika, thyme, sage and cayenne pepper. Drop in cubed beef, a little at a time. Holding the bag tightly closed, shake vigorously. Remove coated pieces and repeat until all beef is coated. Set aside.

In a saucepan, bring water to a boil. Add Worcestershire sauce, bouillon cubes, onion soup mix, wine, bay leaf, parsley, lemon juice, salt, horseradish and Pickapeppa sauce. Turn off heat and let mixture stand.

Heat residual oil in Dutch oven. Brown coated beef a little at a time and set aside. Add diced yellow onion, garlic, sliced pepperoni and mushrooms to oil; sauté until onions become translucent. Mix in browned beef and pork; stir in bouillon mixture. Bring mixture to a boil, then lower heat, cover and simmer for 30 minutes.

Uncover stew and add white onions, potatoes and carrots, stirring well. Cover and simmer for 1½ hours. Uncover stew, stir and simmer uncovered for an additional 30 minutes. Serve on a bed of Poppied Noodles.

Yields: Six to eight servings.

Beef, Pork and Lamb

Riverdale's Liver with Bacon and Mushrooms

Unfortunately, not everyone can find the pleasure I do when dining on liver. For those who love liver—and for those who can abide it once or twice a year—this is a meal you can really enjoy.

This meal is excellent with Woodhaven's Minted Peas.

½ c. butter or margarine
1 lg. onion, peeled and thinly sliced
½ lb. fresh mushrooms, washed and sliced
2 lbs. calf liver, cut into bite-size cubes
½ lb. bacon, cooked and crumbled
salt and pepper to taste

Melt butter or margarine in a large skillet. Add onions and mushrooms; sauté until both are soft, about 5 minutes. Add liver and bacon; cook until liver loses its red color. Sprinkle with salt and pepper to taste and cover. Heat for 2 minutes. Turn off heat, uncover and let stand for 1 minute before serving.

Yields: Four servings.

Beef, Pork and Lamb

Coney Island Hamburgers

These hamburgers are fun—just like Coney Island itself. They may look like other hamburgers, but, as we all know, things aren't always what they appear to be.

2½ lbs. lean ground beef
4 bacon strips, cooked and crumbled
1 sm. potato, peeled and grated
1 sm. onion, peeled and diced
1 egg
¼ c. bread crumbs
¼ c. water
2 lg. garlic cloves, peeled and crushed
1 tsp. Worcestershire sauce
1 tsp. salt
1 tsp. soy sauce
⅛ tsp. cayenne pepper

In a large bowl, combine all ingredients, mix thoroughly and shape into 12 hamburger patties.

These burgers are best barbecued, but they can also be broiled in your oven. When cooking, do not turn over for 3 to 5 minutes, as they tend to fall apart.

Serve with a platter of sliced tomatoes and Red Devil onions on a bed of lettuce leaves. And toasted English muffins leave all the so-called hamburger rolls at the post.

Yields: Twelve servings.

Beef, Pork and Lamb

Laurelton Reuben Casserole

1 16-oz. can sauerkraut, drained
1 med. onion, peeled and diced
1 tsp. caraway seed
1 lb. Swiss cheese, cubed
1 lb. cooked corned beef, cut in 2-inch strips
1 c. blue cheese dressing (for Bayside's Blue Cheese Dressing)
2 c. rye bread, cubed (about 5 slices)
¼ c. unsalted butter, melted

Preheat oven to 375 degrees.

Mix sauerkraut thoroughly with diced onion and caraway seed. In a large baking pan sprayed with a non-stick spray coating, evenly distribute the sauerkraut mixture. Cover with half the Swiss cheese, half the corned beef and half the blue cheese dressing; then the remaining corned beef, the remaining Swiss cheese and the remaining blue cheese dressing. Top the casserole with rye bread cubes and drizzle with melted butter.

Bake for 35 minutes. Serve with salad.

Yields: Six servings.

Beef, Pork and Lamb

Beef, Pork and Lamb

East Village Chili on Cornbread

The East Village has always been the bubbly part of New York's melting pot. Since you can make this chili as hot as you like and it is also a melting pot of the best ingredients of every regional chili recipe you can think of, I can't think of a better neighborhood to name it after.

½ c. Chianti
½ c. water
2 tbs. chili powder
2 tsp. salt
½ tsp. oregano
½ tsp. cumin seeds
1 tsp. fennel seeds
½ tsp. sage
½ tsp. cayenne pepper
½ tsp. dried mint leaves
1 tbs. Pickapeppa sauce (or steak sauce of your choice)
2 tbs. chocolate syrup
3 lbs. lean ground beef
1 med. yellow onion, peeled and chopped
6 garlic cloves, peeled and crushed
12 pepperoncini peppers, cleaned, stemmed and cut in half lengthwise
60 oz. canned kidney beans
1 28-oz. can crushed tomatoes
½ c. chopped pepperoni
½ c. shallots, peeled and chopped

In a large measuring cup, combine Chianti, water, chili powder, salt, oregano, cumin and fennel seeds, sage, cayenne pepper, mint leaves, Pickapeppa sauce and chocolate syrup; mix well.

Beef, Pork and Lamb

In a Dutch oven, brown ground beef, onions and garlic; drain off excess fat. Add peppers, juice from kidney beans, tomatoes, pepperoni, shallots and seasoning sauce. Bring mixture to a boil, then lower heat and simmer, covered, for 45 minutes. Stir in kidney beans and simmer for an additional 15 minutes.

Cornbread:

2 7-oz. boxes corn muffin mix
2 eggs
²/₃ c. milk

Prepare cornbread according to package directions, baking in a shallow roasting pan. When cornbread is ready, cut into squares for individual servings. Place one square on each plate and cover with a generous ladle of chili.

Yields: Ten servings

Beef, Pork and Lamb

Marinated London Broil

As with the Glendale Pot Roast, this recipe is no longer prepared in Big Apple firehouses. This is okay, however, because as with all firehouse recipes, it is well received at home or at neighborhood barbecues.

2 2-lb. london broil steaks
meat tenderizer
⅓ c. Chianti wine
¼ c. soy sauce
3 tbs. Worcestershire sauce
3 tbs. lemon juice
1 tsp. garlic powder
½ tsp. onion powder
½ tsp. oregano
½ tsp. basil
½ tsp. parsley
½ tsp. salt
⅛ tsp. powdered mustard
2 cans beer
⅓ c. onion flakes

Place steaks in a shallow baking pan; sprinkle both sides with meat tenderizer. Thoroughly pierce steaks on both sides with a fork. Combine all ingredients, except beer and onion flakes, and rub this spice paste over steaks. Let stand for at least 10 minutes. Pour beer over steaks and cover with onion flakes. After 20 minutes, turn steaks and ladle onion flakes on top of steaks again. Let stand for another 20 minutes, basting occasionally.

Steaks can either be barbecued or broiled, but the important thing to remember is to baste the meat with marinade.

Yields: Six to eight servings.

Beef, Pork and Lamb

Beef, Pork and Lamb

Chinese Sauerbraten

The FDNY enjoys an unusually beautiful working chart, which makes the vacation schedule (only one scheduled during the summer months every four years) tolerable.

The chart calls for two 15-hour night tours followed by 72 hours off and then two 9-hour day tours followed by 48 hours off. Once a month this 48-hour swing is extended to 72 hours (don't worry — it all works out to 40 hours a week) and is called a Chinese 72.

That is the extent of the Chinese influence in this recipe. I first came across this recipe when I asked a firehouse cook why he was taking so much trouble for lunch. It seems that he prepared the marinade on the eve of his Chinese 72 and his fellow cooks, working while he's off, stir the marinade twice a day until he returns for his first night tour and completes the recipe.

Now for the recipe:

1½ c. Burgandy
1½ c. red wine vinegar
1 lg. Bermuda onion, chopped
1 carrot, chopped
4 lg. bay leaves
1½ tbs. pickling spice
1 tsp. celery salt
1 tbs. black peppercorns
4 to 5 lbs. cubed rump roast
1 lb. bacon, sliced into cubes, divided
4 tbs. peanut oil (olive oil can be substituted)
½ c. whole wheat flour & brown paper bag
2 8-oz. cans College Inn beef broth
1 8-oz. jar of cocktail onions
½ c. crushed gingersnap cookies (or to taste)

Beef, Pork and Lamb

To prepare: Bring wine and vinegar to a boil, remove from stove and allow mixture to cool. Pour mixture into a large stainless steel bowl, add onion, carrot, bay leaves, pickling spice, celery salt, peppercorns and rump roast. Cover and refrigerate for a Chinese 72. Marinade should be stirred twice a day for 3 days

To cook: Remove meat from marinade and allow to drain in a colander. Reserve marinade. Cook bacon in a large saucepan until crisp. Remove and drain on paper towels. Discard bacon grease. Add peanut oil to the pan. Put flour in bag, add drained meat and shake to coat evenly. Now add coated meat to pan in manageable amounts and brown on all sides, removing as necessary, until it's all done. Pour entire marinade mixture and beef broth into pan and bring to a boil. As mixture is heating, use a wooden spoon and scrape the bottom of the pan to free up those delicious bits stuck to the bottom. Then lower flame to a simmer and add meat and cocktail onions, and cook partially covered for about 1 hour—until meat is tender. Using a slotted spoon, remove meat and vegetables and add crushed gingersnaps and bacon, stirring until they dissolve into the sauce. Then return meat and vegetables, mix well and serve.

Yields: Eight to ten servings.

Beef, Pork and Lamb

Gramercy Park Meat Loaf

You are going to love this meat loaf because, like its namesake, it is unique to its surroundings. This recipe should be served with Finger-lickin' Mashed Potatoes and Wall Street Spinach Salad.

1 sm. onion, peeled and diced
3 lbs. lean ground beef
1½ c. seasoned bread crumbs
¾ c. water
2 eggs
1 tbs. ketchup
1 tbs. Worcestershire sauce
1 tbs. fresh chopped parsley
½ tsp. hickory-smoked salt
½ tsp. horseradish
⅛ tsp. powdered mustard
⅛ tsp. cayenne pepper
¼ c. burgundy wine
½ tsp. bacon bits
⅛ tsp. sage
1 tsp. Pickapeppa sauce (or steak sauce of your choice)
1 garlic clove, peeled and crushed

Preheat oven to 350 degrees.

Combine all ingredients, mixing well. In a shallow baking pan, shape mixture like a football and cut in half lengthwise. This shape allows meat to be cooked in varying degrees of doneness, from well done to medium. Bake for 1 hour and 15 minutes.

This mixture also makes excellent hamburgers.

Yields: Six to eight servings.

Beef, Pork and Lamb

Gourmet Irish Brisket

½ c. maple syrup
½ c. brown sugar
3 tsp. Dijon mustard
1 tsp. peach, apple or raspberry preserves
1 tsp. pickling spice
½ tsp. red pepper flakes
¼ tsp. nutmeg
¼ tsp. cinnamon
¼ tsp. dried mint leaves
1 3-4 lb. corned beef brisket
2 carrots, peeled and cut into thirds
6 potatoes, peeled and halved

Preheat oven to 350 degrees.

Combine syrup, sugar, mustard, preserves and seasonings to form glaze. Place brisket and glaze in a plastic bag for one hour, turning and mixing every 15 minutes.

Remove brisket from bag and place on a rack in a 2-inch deep baking pan. Fill pan with water up to the top of the rack. Cover tightly with aluminum foil. Bake for 1 hour.

Remove pan from oven and add carrots and potatoes. Pour ⅓ reserved glaze over brisket; re-cover and bake for 2 hours, checking occasionally. When brisket is fork-tender, uncover roasting pan, drain all liquid from the bottom and pour the remaining glaze on top. Return pan to oven and bake uncovered for 15 more minutes.

Yields: Eight to ten servings.

Beef, Pork and Lamb

Firehouse Italian Meatballs

If you enjoy company, just let the word out that you're serving Firehouse Meatballs.

1½ lbs. lean ground beef
¾ c. seasoned Italian bread crumbs
½ c. water
1 egg
2 tbs. fresh chopped parsley
2 tbs. Parmesan cheese
1 tsp. garlic powder
½ tsp. salt

In a large bowl, thoroughly mix all ingredients together. Shape into meatballs. Add to a boiling pot of Elizabeth Street Spaghetti Sauce. Do not stir sauce for 10 minutes after adding meatballs. When sauce returns to a boil, lower heat and simmer for about 2 hours. Every 20 minutes or so, skim excess fat off top of sauce and stir well. The meatballs will be cooked in 1 hour, but they can stay in the sauce for as long as it simmers.

Yields:

Beef, Pork and Lamb

Italian Braciole

For some reason, braciole is generally considered a delicacy in spaghetti sauce. While I was preparing it on a night tour, one of my helpers said, "You mean that's all there is to making braciole? You coulda' fooled me." This recipe may be simple, but its effect is outrageous.

3 slices prosciutto, diced
2 tbs. Parmesan cheese
1 tbs. chopped fresh parsley
$1/8$ tsp. onion powder
$1/8$ tsp. salt
$1/8$ tsp. garlic powder
dash black pepper
$3/4$ c. seasoned Italian bread crumbs
6 pieces round steak, pounded for braciole

Combine prosciutto with cheese, parsley, onion powder, salt, garlic powder, pepper and bread crumbs; mix well. In the center of each piece of round steak, place 3 or 4 tbs. prosciutto mixture. Roll steak in jelly-roll fashion and secure with a toothpick at each end. Repeat process until all six pieces of round steak are rolled.

Add braciole to a pot of boiling Elizabeth Street Spaghetti Sauce. Do not stir sauce for 10 minutes. When sauce returns to a boil, lower heat and simmer for about 2 hours. Every 20 minutes or so, skim excess fat from top of sauce and stir sauce well. The braciole will be thoroughly cooked in 1 hour but they can stay in the sauce for as long as it simmers.

Yields: Six servings.

Beef, Pork and Lamb

Ridgewood's Fresh Ham

Most Americans are familiar with the versatility of fresh ham. The following recipe is a precise blend of spices that brings this historic American favorite to its full potential.

1 5-8 lb. fresh ham (with bone)
1 oz. Rhine wine
1 tsp. maple syrup
½ tsp. Worcestershire sauce
½ tsp. Dijon mustard
½ tsp. onion powder
½ tsp. salt
½ tsp. nutmeg
½ tsp. grated lemon peel
½ tsp. cinnamon
⅛ tsp. sage
⅛ tsp. cayenne pepper
dash ground cloves and ginger, to taste
⅛ tsp. garlic powder

Preheat oven to 450 degrees.

Wash ham and pat dry. Cut a pocket in the outer skin towards top half of roast. In a measuring cup, combine remaining ingredients, except garlic powder; mix well. With a carving fork, pierce roast all over. Rub seasoning mixture all over ham, pouring excess into the pocket.

Place ham in a roasting pan. Dust top with garlic powder. Cover with aluminum foil to prevent outside from cooking too quickly. Bake for 30 minutes. Lower oven temperature to 350 degrees and cook 35 minutes per pound. One hour before ham is ready, remove foil. Let stand for 15 to 20 minutes before carving.

After the meal is over, save the bone for JFK Pea Soup.

Yields: Four to six servings.

Beef, Pork and Lamb

Apples 'n Pork Chops

Long before anyone thought of coupling New York City with the apple—big or otherwise—firehouse cooks had already married apples and pork chops. Try this delicious recipe and step back in time.

¼ c. butter or margarine
2 lg. apples, washed, cored and sliced
1 lg. onion, peeled and thinly sliced
1 10¾-oz. can condensed cream of mushroom soup
¼ c. Rhine wine
3-4 lbs. pork chops (about 6-8 chops)

Preheat oven to 325 degrees.

In a skillet, melt butter or margarine. Add apple and onion slices. Sauté until onion is soft. Add soup and wine to skillet, mix well and heat through.

In a baking pan coated with a non-stick spray coating, arrange pork chops and cover with apple mixture. Bake for about 90 minutes, depending on thickness of chops.

Yields: Six to eight servings.

Beef, Pork and Lamb

Beef, Pork and Lamb

Christmas Cherried Ham

This festive recipe shouldn't be saved just for Christmas, *but* it should be saved for those three or four special occasions that occur during the year.

1 5-lb. canned ham, fully cooked
¼ c. Rhine wine
¼ c. orange juice
1 5-oz. jar apple jelly
3 tbs. maple syrup
1 tbs. Dijon mustard
1 tsp. soy sauce
¼ c. lemon juice
1 16-oz. can pitted tart cherries

Preheat oven to 325 degrees.

Place ham on a rack in a shallow baking pan and bake for 90 minutes. Fifteen minutes before ham is ready, place remaining ingredients, except cherries, in a saucepan and bring to a boil. Lower heat and simmer for about 10 minutes, then add cherries, juice and all, mixing well. Continue to simmer.

Remove ham from oven and make diagonal cuts approximately 1-inch deep in a diamond pattern on top of ham. Generously ladle sauce only (no cherries) over ham. Make sure it gets deeply into ham. Save cherries and remaining sauce.

Return coated ham to oven for 30 minutes. Then ladle cherries and remaining sauce over ham and return to oven for 15 minutes. Remove from oven and let stand for 15 minutes for easy slicing.

Yields: Eight to ten servings.

Beef, Pork and Lamb

Hawaiian Ham Steaks

Like everyone, firefighters dream. This recipe was created on the spur of the moment when someone started dreaming out loud about winning the Irish Sweepstakes (you remember, before we had state lotteries!) and going to Hawaii. This "When I Win Recipe" has little to do with Hawaii except what the firehouse cook imagined as he combined his ingredients. So just close your eyes, open your mouth ... and dream.

1 5-lb. boneless smoked ham, cooked and sliced
    into ½-inch thick steaks
1 20-oz. can crushed pineapple
⅓ c. orange juice
1 tsp. maple syrup
1 tsp. Dijon mustard
1 tsp. brown sugar
½ tsp. lemon juice
½ tsp. soy sauce
⅛ tsp. ground cinnamon
⅛ tsp. ground nutmeg
dash ground cloves
dash cayenne pepper

Preheat oven to 350 degrees.

Arrange ham steaks into two or three roasting pans which have been coated with a non-stick spray coating.

In a mixing bowl, combine remaining ingredients, mixing well. Ladle sauce over ham steaks and bake for 30 minutes.

Yields: Six to eight servings.

Beef, Pork and Lamb

Soul Ribs

A certain bond, almost a love, develops between firefighters and those they serve. People try to show their appreciation for the sacrifices and efforts they see expended on their behalf. This recipe was passed on to a neighborhood firehouse just to say "thanks." Unpretentious Cole Slaw sets these ribs off perfectly.

6 lbs. country-style pork ribs
1 c. ketchup
¼ c. rosé wine
2 tbs. soy sauce
2 tbs. maple syrup
2 tbs. lemon juice
2 tbs. brown sugar
1 tsp. Dijon mustard

Preheat oven to 400 degrees.

Separate ribs into individual pieces; arrange in baking dishes which have been coated with a non-stick spray coating.

In a small bowl, combine remaining ingredients, mixing thoroughly. With a basting brush, coat ribs with sauce, bake for 30 minutes, then lower oven temperature to 350 degrees and bake for an additional hour. Turn and baste ribs every 15 to 20 minutes while cooking.

Yields: Four servings.

Flatbush Roast Leg O' Lamb

The Boys of Summer may be long gone to Dodgers Stadium in Los Angeles, but as this recipe clearly shows, "Da Pride 'a Flatbush" lives on. This meal goes very well with Woodhaven's Minted Peas.

1 c. burgundy wine
1 tbs. lemon juice
2 tsp. Dijon mustard
2 tsp. whole wheat flour
1 tsp. garlic powder
1 tsp. salt
1 tsp. paprika
1 tsp. Worcestershire sauce
½ tsp. onion powder
½ tsp. dried rosemary
⅛ tsp. cayenne pepper
⅛ tsp. sage
⅛ tsp. thyme
1 6-7 lb. leg of lamb, well trimmed
12 new potatoes, peeled
1 lg. Bermuda onion, peeled and thickly sliced
1 c. water

Preheat oven to 350 degrees.

In a measuring cup, combine ½ c. wine, lemon juice, mustard, flour, garlic powder, salt, paprika, Worcestershire sauce, onion powder, rosemary, pepper, sage and thyme. Mix thoroughly.

Pierce lamb with a fork and rub with the wine and herb mixture. Pour any excess over top. Coat a roasting pan with non-stick spray coating and place lamb in center. Arrange potatoes all around the lamb and onion slices on top. Pour remaining wine and herb mixture over top again.

Beef, Pork and Lamb

Roast for 30 minutes, then pour a mixture of ½ c. water and ½ c. burgundy wine on top of meat. Return to oven for 90 minutes. Pour ½ c. water in bottom of roasting pan and continue roasting for another 30 minutes.

Remove lamb from roasting pan and set aside for 5 minutes or so. Place roasted potatoes in a serving dish. Have someone carve the leg of lamb while you make a gravy using roasted onions and drippings.

Yields: Six to eight servings.

Beef, Pork and Lamb

Boro Park Lamb Chops

Every culture has certain subtleties that seem to inhibit culinary pursuits. In the United States, for example, rabbit is rarely enjoyed, even in our most cosmopolitan areas. Yet rabbit is a staple of French cooking!

It has been my experience that we are beginning to lose interest in delicious lamb. I urge you to try one of my favorite recipes *before it's too late.*

6 tbs. whole wheat flour
12 loin lamb chops, trimmed of fat
3 tbs. Dijon mustard
1 tbs. lemon juice
3 oz. Rhine wine
¾ c. bread crumbs
¼ c. cornflake crumbs
2 tbs. onion flakes
2 tbs. chopped fresh parsley
1 tbs. Parmesan cheese
1 tsp. garlic powder
½ tsp. basil
¼ tsp. sage
¼ c. vegetable oil

Preheat oven to 400 degrees.

Place flour in a paper lunchbag. Drop in a chop, hold top tightly closed and shake vigorously. Repeat until all chops are coated.

In a measuring cup, mix mustard, lemon juice and wine into a sauce; set aside. In a small bowl combine bread crumbs, cornflake crumbs, onion flakes, parsley, Parmesan cheese, garlic powder, basil and sage

Beef, Pork and Lamb

In a skillet, heat oil and lightly brown chops on both sides. With a basting brush, lightly coat chops on both sides with Dijon-wine mix. Roll in crumb mix. Place chops in a large baking pan coated with a non-stick spray coating and bake for 15 minutes or until golden. Turn chops and return to oven for 15 minutes.

Yields: Twelve servings.

Bowery Pork Taters 'n' Kraut Casserole

From the day when rare pinto horses answered the call of "fire" in lower Manhattan, this recipe has been a favorite in Big Apple firehouses.

2 tbs. vegetable oil
3-4 lbs. pork chops (about 6 to 8 chops)
6 med. potatoes, washed, peeled and sliced
1 16-oz. can sauerkraut, drained
1 can beer

In a Dutch oven, heat oil and brown chops on both sides. Remove chops and set aside. Cover bottom of Dutch oven with a layer of pork chops, then a layer of potato slices, and finally a layer of sauerkraut. Repeat this process until everything is used up. Pour beer over all and bring to a boil. Reduce heat, cover and simmer for about 90 minutes, depending on thickness of chops.

Yields: Six to eight servings.

CHICKEN

History buffs will recall that in the Presidential campaign of 1932 that pitted Hoover against FDR, the Republicans tried to rally the American people from the depths of the Depression by promising "A chicken in every pot!"

Despite America's traditional love of chicken, the slogan couldn't overcome the perceived economic hardships of the times. Perhaps, just perhaps, if recipes such as the following were popular at the time, "A chicken in every pot" could have become the rallying cry that changed history. Imagine, a chicken changing destiny!

Chicken

Canarsie's Chicken Cacciatore

Chicken Cacciatore is a delicious escape from the usual fare we face day in and day out—especially if you prepare it firehouse style! If you really want a different fare, broil the chicken according to the recipe and then cook it in the Go For It Garlic Bread Sauce for 20 to 30 minutes. No matter how you prepare the chicken, this recipe is a true pleasure to get into.

Wall Street Spinach Salad is a nice accompaniment to this dish.

1 lg. broiling chicken, cut up
2 tbs. margarine, melted and seasoned with $1/8$ tsp. garlic powder and $1/8$ tsp. onion powder
$1/4$ c. Chianti wine
2 tbs. fresh chopped parsley
1 tsp. salt
2 tbs. grated Parmesan cheese
2 lg. onions, peeled and chopped
$1/4$ c. olive oil
3 lg. garlic cloves, peeled and crushed
1 tsp. basil
$1/2$ tsp. oregano
$1/2$ tsp. Italian red pepper flakes
1 28-oz. can crushed tomatoes
1 28-oz. can tomato puree
1 28-oz. can water
$1/2$ lb. fresh mushrooms, cleaned and halved
1 lb. macaroni (I prefer Ronzoni Rigatoni #27)

Place chicken pieces in a broiler pan and drizzle with seasoned butter. Broil until skin gets cripsy and golden, about 12 minutes. Remove, drain and set aside.

In a measuring cup, combine wine, parsley, salt and Parmesan cheese.

Chicken

In a large pot, sauté onions in oil until soft. Add garlic, basil, oregano and pepper; sauté another 3 to 5 minutes. Add crushed tomatoes, tomato puree, water, mushrooms, wine and herb mixture and chicken. Bring to a boil, reduce heat and simmer, covered, for about 2 hours. Skim excess fat off top of sauce every 20 minutes or so—this is very important.

About 20 minutes before sauce is done, prepare macaroni according to package directions. Drain macaroni in a colander, then place in a serving bowl. Add 2-4 ladles of sauce to macaroni to prevent it from sticking. Serve macaroni on individual plates generously topped with the cacciatore.

Yields: Six servings.

Chicken

Chinatown Chicken and Vegetables

No accounting of New York City's special cultural delicacies would be complete without acknowledging the contributions of our Chinese citizens. They have given the Big Apple a special ambiance, a sense of family, and most obviously a special cuisine. We are richer culturally because of their influence. This recipe, I believe, demonstrates this rich and tasty influence.
Side Car Rice is perfect with this dish.

1 c. fresh bean sprouts
4 chicken cutlets
¼ c. water
¼ c. Rhine wine
¼ tsp. garlic powder
¼ tsp. paprika
¼ tsp. allspice
⅛ tsp. salt
⅛ tsp. ground ginger
1 tbs. lemon juice
¼ c. soy sauce
1 tsp. arrowroot or cornstarch
4 tbs. vegetable oil
1 lg. onion, peeled and sliced
1 box frozen broccoli
1 red bell pepper, washed, cored and thinly sliced
¼ lb. fresh radishes, washed and sliced
½ lb. fresh mushrooms, washed and halved

Soak bean sprouts in cold water to make them crispy. Cut chicken cutlets into bite-size pieces. In a shallow bowl, combine water, wine, garlic powder, paprika, allspice, salt, ginger and lemon juice. Add chicken pieces and mix well. In a measuring cup, mix soy sauce and arrowroot or cornstarch.

Chicken

In a large skillet, heat 2 tbs. oil and brown drained chicken pieces; remove and set aside. Heat remaining oil in skillet and add wine and spice sauce, sliced onion, broccoli, bell pepper, radishes and mushrooms. Stir-fry for 3 to 5 minutes, until vegetables are heated through but not wilted. Stir in drained bean sprouts, chicken pieces and soy-arrowroot mixture; cook until gravy thickens. Serve over rice.

Yields: Six to eight servings.

Chicken

Spiced Garden Chicken

1 8-oz. can College Inn chicken broth
2 oz. Rhine wine
2 tsp. lemon juice
1 tsp. pure anise extract
½ tsp. fennel seed
½ tsp. cumin seed
½ tsp. salt
¼ tsp. nutmeg
¼ tsp. powdered dill
¼ tsp. thyme
¼ tsp. tarragon
⅛ tsp. cayenne pepper
4 tbs. peanut oil
3 lbs. chicken cutlets, cubed
1 lg. yellow onion, peeled and sliced into rings
2 lg. cloves garlic, crushed
1 lg. red bell pepper, seeded and cut into strips
1 lg. yellow bell pepper, seeded and cut into strips
1 sm. green bell pepper, seeded and cut into strips

In a large saucepan with a cover, bring chicken broth to a boil. Continue until slightly reduced. Lower heat to simmer, and add wine, lemon juice, and all the spices. Cover and simmer for 20 minutes. In a large skillet, heat the oil and sauté cutlets until golden, approximately 2-3 minutes on each side. Remove and set aside. Add more oil if necessary, and stir-fry the vegetables, beginning with onion until translucent, then add the garlic until golden, then the peppers and stir-fry approximately 3 minutes. Now return the chicken and continue to stir-fry for an additional 2 to 3 minutes. Uncover spiced chicken broth, bring to a boil, and add chicken and vegetables. Re-cover saucepan and continue cooking for 15 minutes.

Yields: Four to six servings.

Chicken

Crummy Chicken

Overheard after a night tour roll call:
"Crummy Chicken again!"
"Yes, because it's *easy!*"
"Yes, because it's *tasty!*"
"Yes, because *you love it!*"
This chicken goes great with Finger-lickin' Mashed Potatoes and G.I. Spiced Peas.

1 egg, beaten with 1 tbs. water
¼ c. Rhine wine
1 tbs. horseradish
¼ c. mayonnaise
1 tbs. Dijon mustard
1 c. seasoned Italian bread crumbs
1 c. cornflake crumbs
2 tbs. sesame seeds
¼ tsp. onion powder
¼ tsp. paprika
¼ tsp. marjoram
½ tsp. salt
¼ tsp. tarragon
pinch cayenne pepper
2 chickens, cut up

Preheat oven to 375 degrees.

In a measuring cup, combine beaten egg mixture, wine, horseradish, mayonnaise and mustard; mix thoroughly.

In a bowl, thoroughly mix all dry ingredients. Dip chicken pieces in egg mixture and then coat with crumb mixture

Place chicken pieces skin-side up in two baking pans coated with a non-stick spray coating. Bake for 45 minutes, then turn and bake an additional 15 minutes, or until crispy.

Yields: Six to eight servings.

Chicken

Old MacDonald's Chicken

This dish gives three delicious flavors to chicken and will bring the most reluctant appetite to the table *early!* When served with Wall Street Spinach Salad or Central Park Salad it makes a beautifully balanced meal. Pork cutlets make an interesting variation.

4 lbs. of chicken cutlets

Sauce #1 — 3 oz. each: red wine vinegar, peanut oil, horseradish, deli mustard, and Dijon mustard
    3 shallots, diced

Sauce #2 — 4 oz. lemon juice
    3 cloves garlic, crushed
    1 tsp. dried mint
    1 shallot, diced
    ½ tsp. salt
    ¼ tsp. cayenne pepper

Sauce #3 — 8 oz. orange juice
    2 tbs. peanut oil
    2 oz. red wine vinegar
    2 oz. soy sauce
    2 oz. honey
    ½ tsp. ginger
    ⅛ tsp. cayenne pepper
    1 shallot, diced
    2 tbs. raspberry conserves

Combine ingredients for each sauce in separate bowls. Add ⅓ of cutlets to each bowl, mix well, cover and let stand for 1 to 2 hours.

Remove coated cutlets. Save mixture for basting.

Broil 3 minutes on each side, basting as necessary. Leftover sauces can be saved for another time.

Yields: Six to eight servings.

Chicken

SEAFOOD

Seafood recipes abound in every culture fortunate enough to be located near the sea, or even near one of its outlets.

The Big Apple is unique among the great ports of the world because most of the city is surrounded by water. Furthering New York's good fortune is the fact that so many immigrants from all corners of the world came to our city and blessed us with a unique variety of tastes and smells that have become a part of our very fiber.

You only have to visit us to see our fascination with the sea and its bounty. Come enjoy the variety of our history by exploring these recipes.

Seafood

No Holds Barred Baked Clams

¼ lb. bacon, diced
2 doz. raw cherrystone clams, on half shell
2 oz. peanut oil
2 oz. Rhine wine
4 tbs. butter, chopped
¾ c. unseasoned bread crumbs
2 cloves garlic, crushed
2 shallots, minced
1 tsp. fresh lemon juice
1 tsp. parsley
1 tsp. basil
½ tsp. oregano
½ tsp. cayenne pepper
2 tbs. freshly ground Romano cheese
*1 3-oz. bottle clam juice — if needed

Cook diced bacon until translucent. Remove and drain on paper towels. Scrub, wash and open clams. Discard unused half of shell. In a blender, combine oil, wine, butter, bread crumbs and all other ingredients, except for bacon and Romano cheese. Blend until smooth and creamy. (If mixture is not moist enough, add some bottled clam juice, one ounce at a time as needed, not too much.) Cover clams with mixture, sprinkle cheese over the top and cover with a piece of bacon. Bake at 450 degrees for 5 or 6 minutes.

Yields: Four to six servings.

Seafood

Seafood

City Hall Shrimp Scampi

City Hall is where "the boss" works. When this recipe was first served, one of the Brothers said, "This is good enough to serve the boss." Thus, the name. This makes an exciting first course, especially when served as a prelude to Whitestone Clam Sauce and spaghetti. You can also serve it as an entree by increasing the portions.

1 lb. fresh raw shrimp
1 c. sweet butter
1 tsp. cornflake crumbs
6 lg. garlic cloves, peeled and crushed
$\frac{1}{2}$ tsp. salt
$\frac{1}{8}$ tsp. cayenne pepper
2 tbs. chopped fresh parsley
$\frac{1}{4}$ c. dry white wine
1 tsp. lemon juice
1 tsp. grated lemon peel
2 fresh lemons, cut into wedges

Preheat oven to 400 degrees.

Shell and devein shrimp, then wash thoroughly. In a saucepan, melt butter and add cornflake crumbs, garlic, salt, cayenne pepper and 1 tbs. parsley. Sauté for 2-3 minutes, add wine, then continue cooking for an additional 3 minutes. Pour $\frac{1}{3}$ butter mixture into a 9×13 baking dish, tilting to coat. Arrange shrimp in a single layer in baking dish and pour remaining butter over top.

Bake shrimp, uncovered, for 5 minutes. Turn and sprinkle with lemon juice, lemon peel and remaining parsley. Return shrimp to oven for 8 to 10 minutes. Serve on a bed of Sidecar Rice.

Yields: Four servings.

Seafood

Sheepshead Bay Mussels

3 lbs. mussels
1 sm. onion, peeled and diced
1 sm. garlic clove, peeled and crushed
1 c. dry white wine
1 tbs. chopped fresh parsley
½ tsp. salt
dash cayenne pepper
4 tbs. butter or margarine

Scrub mussels, removing any foreign matter. Set up two large pots, one filled with ice water, the other with water at room temperature. Place mussels in ice water for 15 minutes. Remove and place in room-temperature water for 5 minutes, then return to ice water for 10 minutes. Once more, remove to fresh room temperature water for another 10 minutes. This procedure speeds the mussels along in expelling any foreign matter they've been hiding inside their shells.

Place mussels in a large kettle with remaining ingredients, reserving 2 tbs. butter or margarine. Cover and boil until mussels open, about 8 minutes. Carefully pour off stock without disturbing sediment. Place stock and remaining 2 tbs. butter in a saucepan and boil until reduced to about 3 c. Discard empty halves of shells. Distribute equal portions of mussels in individual soup bowls. Cover with reduced stock and serve piping hot.

Yields: Four to six servings.

Seafood

Redhook Paella

This recipe is the Rolls Royce of Hispanic cuisine. It is more than worth all the effort it calls for — believe me!

2 chickens, cut up into small pieces
$1/_8$ tsp. garlic powder
$1/_8$ tsp. onion powder
2 tsp. paprika
2 lbs. black mussels
12 cherrystone clams
4 tbs. olive oil
4 lg. onions, peeled and diced
4 garlic cloves, peeled and diced
1 red bell pepper, washed, cored and thinly sliced
2 oz. pepperoni, peeled and diced
1 lb. fresh mushrooms, washed and halved
¼ c. water
¼ c. Rhine wine
1 10¼-oz. can minced clams
1 6-oz. can minced crabmeat
1 tsp. Worcestershire sauce
1 tsp. lemon juice
½ tsp. saffron
3 13¾-oz. cans chicken broth
2 c. long grain rice
1 box frozen baby peas
1 sm. jar roasted red peppers, thinly sliced

Arrange chicken skin-side up in an oven broiler tray coated with a non-stick spray coating. Sprinkle with garlic powder, onion powder and 1 tsp. paprika. Broil chicken until skin is golden and crispy, about 6 to 8 minutes. Wash, scrub and soak mussels and cherrystones in cold water.

Seafood

In a very large pot, heat olive oil and add onion, sautéing until soft. Add garlic, red bell pepper and pepperoni; cook for 3 to 5 minutes. Remove chicken from broiler, turn, coat with remaining 1 tsp. paprika and return to broiler until golden and crispy, about 5 minutes. Stir mushrooms, water and wine into pot and bring to a boil. Lower heat and simmer, adding minced clams, crabmeat, Worcestershire sauce and lemon juice; stir well. Remove chicken from broiler, drain and add to pot, along with saffron and chicken broth; stir well and bring to a boil. Lower heat and simmer, mixing in rice.

Cover and simmer over very low heat until chicken and rice are cooked, about 20 minutes, stirring occasionally. Add shellfish, pushing clams and mussels down into rice and gravy. Cook until clams open, about 15 minutes. Then stir in frozen peas and roasted red pepper, re-cover and continue cooking for 2 to 3 minutes.

Yields: Eight to ten servings.

Seafood

Cioppino D'Amore

For most New Yorkers, an evening at an Italian restaurant is a favorite night out. Unfortunately, most of the earthy aromas are left in the restaurant. This recipe will permeate your home to the point where you and your loved one will be enticed to hum, if not sing *"Arrivederci Roma."* Enjoy!

1 lb. bacon cut crosswise into ½" pieces
2 tbs. olive oil
2 sweet red bell peppers diced into ½" pieces
1 Bermuda onion, diced
1 leek, cleaned and diced
6 cloves garlic, peeled and crushed
3 c. chicken stock
3 c. clam juice
2 c. red table wine
4 c. canned tomatoes
⅛ tsp. saffron
¼ tsp. cayenne pepper
1 tsp. fennel seed
1 tsp. each: oregano, dried basil, dried thyme, parsley and dill
3 lg. bay leaves
1 sm. fresh jalapeno pepper, seeded and chopped (do this under running water)
Grated zest of 1 lemon
salt and pepper to taste
2 lbs. sea bass or any other firm white-fleshed fish, cut into 1" pieces
1 6-oz. can conch, drained and chopped
1 6-oz. can squid, drained and chopped
1 4-oz. can crab, drained
1 doz. littleneck clams, cleaned
1 doz. mussels, cleaned
1 doz. lg. shrimp, cleaned and deveined
1 doz. oysters, cleaned

Seafood

In a large saucepan, cook bacon over medium heat until soft. Remove the bacon grease from the pan. Return the pan to heat, add the oil, red pepper, onion and leek. Cook about 5 minutes, stirring occasionally, add crushed garlic and cook until garlic is golden. Meanwhile, add the chicken stock, clam juice, wine, tomatoes, spices and chopped jalapeno pepper. Bring to a boil and simmer for 30-40 minutes (until liquid is reduced by around $1/3$).

Add the seafood and lemon zest. Mix well and cook for an additional 5-6 minutes or until clams open. Stir gently, salt and pepper to taste, and allow cioppino to rest for 3-5 minutes before serving.

Yields: Six to eight servings.

Seafood

Seafood

N'Orleans Fried Fish

This recipe, while in the Cajun style, uses a blend of spices that reaches far beyond the expected. It is more U.N. than Cajun.

2 lbs. fluke fillets rinsed (flounder, sea bass, or comparable fish can also be used)
½ c. whole wheat flour
½ c. cornflake crumbs
1 tsp. celery salt
1 tsp. basil
½ tsp. oregano
½ tsp. chile powder
½ tsp. cayenne powder
¼ tsp. curry powder
¼ tsp. garlic powder
¼ tsp. onion powder
2 eggs beaten with 2 tsp. white wine
peanut oil as needed

Combine flour, cornflake crumbs and all the spices. Mix well. Dip fillets in egg mixture and dredge through spiced flour/crumb mixture. Heat oil in a large frying pan. When it is hot, begin frying fillets. Fillets should be cooked until crispy golden on each side, approximately 3-4 minutes.

Yields: Four to six servings.

Seafood New York

This recipe brings the full richness of New York and marries it with the treasures of the sea. It is a meal that will be enjoyed by seafood lovers who appreciate a rich and slightly Italian background.

1 c. ricotta cheese
1 c. plain yogurt
½ c. dry white wine
¼ c. grated Parmesan cheese
3 tbs. Worcestershire sauce
½ tsp. salt
dash cayenne pepper
4 tbs. sweet butter
1 sm. onion, peeled and thinly sliced
1 lg. garlic clove, peeled and crushed
½ lb. fresh mushrooms, washed and halved
6 oz. frozen crabmeat, thawed
6 oz. frozen shrimp, thawed
1 6-oz. can minced clams
1 lb. fresh bay scallops
2 c. cooked rice
¼ c. bread crumbs
¼ c. cornflake crumbs

Preheat oven to 350 degrees.

In a small bowl, combine ricotta, yogurt, wine, Parmesan cheese, Worcestershire sauce, salt and pepper; mix well. In a large skillet, melt 2 tbs. butter. Add onions, garlic and mushrooms; sauté until onion is soft, about 5 minutes. Add seafood and simmer for 5 minutes. Stir in ricotta mixture and cooked rice, heat for 2 to 3 minutes. Melt remaining butter and add bread and cornflake crumbs, mixing well.

Seafood

Place seafood mixture into a large casserole coated with a non-stick spray coating and cover with crumb mix. Bake at 350 degrees for about 30 minutes.

Yields: Six to eight servings.

Joyful Salmon Cakes

When served with Wall Street Spinach Salad or Central Park Salad, this delicious recipe enthralls even the most sophisticated palate.

1 med. onion, chopped
1 egg, beaten
1 lg. can salmon or tuna
1 tbs. basil
1 tbs. parsley
1 tbs. black pepper
1 c. bread crumbs
½ c. shredded cheddar cheese
1 oz. oil

Mix all ingredients together — except for ½ of the bread crumbs. Form patties about the size of your palm. Coat patties with the remaining bread crumbs. Fry in heated oil until golden brown, approximately 3-4 minutes on each side.

VEGETABLES

Vegetables! The word brings a frown to too many faces. Why? We're all intelligent people—aren't we? In this day of physical fitness, everyone knows the importance of the vegetable. Yet, it usually becomes the "bite the bullet" part of the meal.

I have collected special recipes over the years that make the frequently disliked vegetable into a treat, and in some cases even a meal unto themselves. Try them—you'll like them!

Vegetables

Williamsburg Stuffed Cabbage

This recipe is wrapped in memories of Ellis Island and the Statue of Liberty. Its old-world preparation brings a special, unique warmth to everyone lucky enough to enjoy it.

1 lg. cabbage head
1 lb. lean ground beef
1 egg
1/8 c. uncooked long grain rice
3 tbs. water
1 sm. onion, peeled and diced
1 tsp. salt
2 tbs. vegetable oil
2 med. onions, peeled and thinly sliced
3 8-oz. cans tomato sauce
1/4 c. lemon juice
1/4 c. sugar
1/8 tsp. salt
1/8 tsp. black pepper

Discard outer leaves of cabbage. Trim away cabbage stem about 1/4 inch into head. Place under hot running water and gently separate leaves. Continue this process until a small head of cabbage is left and your efforts only produce tiny leaves. (The unpeeled portion can be used to make Unpretentious Cole Slaw.)

In a mixing bowl, combine ground beef, egg, rice, water, diced onion and 1 tsp. salt; mix well. Place 2 to 3 tbs. filling mixture in the center of each cabbage leaf, tuck in the sides and tightly roll together without losing any filling.

Vegetables

In a Dutch oven, heat oil and add onion slices, sautéing until soft. Stir in tomato sauce, lemon juice, sugar, salt and pepper. Bring to a boil, cover and simmer for 10 minutes. Carefully place each rolled cabbage in sauce, return sauce to a boil, cover and simmer for two hours.

Yields: Six to eight servings.

Vegetables

South Bronx Stuffed Peppers

Everyone has heard of the South Bronx and the fires that ravaged that area. This recipe is my small tribute to the firefighters who fought and fight so heroically in this ravaged area.

1½ c. seasoned Italian bread crumbs
½ c. cornflake crumbs
1 egg
6 oz. Parmesan cheese
6 oz. rosé wine
8 med. red bell peppers
1 lb. lean ground beef
2 med. onions, peeled and diced
2 lg. garlic cloves, peeled and crushed
¼ lb. Genoa salami (about 12 slices), peeled and diced
¼ c. Minute rice
1 c. spaghetti sauce

Preheat oven to 350 degrees.

Mix together bread crumbs, cornflake crumbs, egg, Parmesan cheese and wine. Slice tops off peppers and clean out insides.

In a saucepan, brown ground beef, onions, garlic, salami and rice. Drain off excess fat.

In a large mixing bowl, combine browned meat mixture with bread crumb mixture.

Gently fill each pepper about ¾ full and top with 2 tbs. spaghetti sauce. Place peppers in glass casserole and bake for 45 minutes.

Yields: Eight servings.

Vegetables

Broccoli Vita

This recipe will perk up the veggie tolerance level of any group.

1 lg. bunch fresh broccoli
½ c. butter or margarine, melted
2 tbs. white horseradish
2 tsp. lemon juice
1 tsp. garlic powder
1 tsp. soy sauce
1 chicken bouillon cube, mashed
dash cayenne pepper
4 tsp. grated Romano cheese

Wash broccoli and separate into individual florets. (The thick stem portion of broccoli can be cut away, peeled and sliced in the same manner a carrot is sliced.) In a saucepan, melt butter or margarine and add remaining ingredients, except Romano cheese, mixing well.

Place broccoli in a skillet with a small amount of water (about ¼ c.); bring to a boil. Stir in herb sauce, cover and simmer until broccoli is tender, about 10 minutes. Serve broccoli piping hot, sprinkled with grated Romano cheese.

Yields: Six to eight servings.

Vegetables

Castelton Corners Creamed Carrots and Cauliflower

1 sm. cauliflower head, washed and separated into florets
1 can condensed cream of celery soup
$1/8$ tsp. garlic powder
$1/8$ tsp. onion powder
1 lb. fresh carrots, peeled and sliced

Preheat oven to 350 degrees.

Steam cauliflower until soft. In a saucepan, combine cream of celery soup, garlic and onion powder. Add 3 tbs. water from steamer and heat through.

In a large casserole, combine vegetables and cream sauce. Toss well and bake at 350 degrees for 15 minutes. Serve piping hot.

Yields: Four to six servings.

Vegetables

Vegetables

Midwood's Baked Mushrooms

Culinary sophistication does exist in boroughs other than Manhattan—and the view is much nicer too! When you try this Brooklyn specialty, you'll see just what I mean.

1 lb. fresh mushrooms (the bigger the better)
¼ c. pistachio nuts, shelled and diced
4 lg. bacon strips, cooked and crumbled
2 tsp. cornflake crumbs
1 tsp. wheat germ
1 tsp. chopped fresh parsley
1 tsp. Dijon mustard
1 tsp. lemon juice
1 tsp. Worcestershire sauce

Preheat oven to 350 degrees.

Wash mushrooms and remove stems. Dice six stems and combine with all remaining ingredients. Mix thoroughly.

Gently stuff mushroom caps and place on a cookie sheet.

Bake for 15 minutes.

Yields: Four to six servings.

Vegetables

Vegetables

G.I. Spiced Peas

1 lg. can peas
1 tbs. onion flakes
1 tsp. basil
1 tsp. lemon juice
pinch oregano

Place all ingredients in a saucepan and bring to a boil. Stir well, turn off heat and let stand for 2 to 3 minutes before serving.

Yields: Four servings.

Sidecar Rice

2½ c. water
1 c. long grain rice
2 chicken bouillon cubes
¼ tsp. onion powder
¼ tsp. garlic powder
dash cayenne pepper
2 oz. butter or margarine

Bring water to a boil. Add all ingredients except butter, cover and simmer over very low heat for 30 minutes. Do not stir or even remove cover — just leave it alone! Uncover, stir in butter until melted, and serve immediately.

Yields: Four to six servings.

Vegetables

Red Devil Onions

One day I realized exactly how much I enjoyed those red onions the hotdog vendors of New York's streets dish out. So home I went, and after a while I came up with this recipe. If you've ever enjoyed those vendors' red onions, then you are in for a rare treat. Red Devil Onions are a true asset to hotdogs, sausage, hamburgers, meatloaf, steak and even roast beef. You can freeze any leftovers.

3 lbs. onions, peeled and thickly sliced
3 garlic cloves, peeled and crushed
¼ c. water
¼ c. Chianti wine
¼ c. lemon juice
3 tbs. soy sauce
3 tbs. Worcestershire sauce
1 tbs. chopped fresh parsley
¼ tsp. salt
¼ tsp. oregano
¼ tsp. basil
¼ tsp. dry mustard
¼ tsp. cayenne pepper
dash sage
¾ c. ketchup
1 8-oz. can tomato sauce

Mix all ingredients, except ketchup and tomato sauce, in a larger saucepan. Bring to a boil, lower heat and simmer, covered, for 10 minutes. Stir in ketchup and tomato sauce, re-cover and simmer for 30 minutes, stirring occasionally.

If you omit the ketchup and tomato sauce, you get delicious steamed onions.

Yields:

Vegetables

Vegetables

Parkville Fried Mushrooms

1 lb. fresh mushrooms
1 egg
¼ c. Rhine wine
¼ c. half 'n' half
1½ c. whole wheat flour
½ tsp. paprika
½ tsp. salt
⅛ tsp. cayenne pepper
¼ c. vegetable oil

Wash and discard undesired portions of mushrooms; larger mushrooms should be separated from stems and both portions used. In a small bowl, combine egg, wine and half 'n' half; mix well. In another small bowl, mix flour, paprika, salt and cayenne pepper.

Heat oil in a large skillet. Dip mushrooms in egg mixture and then dredge in flour mixture until well-coated. Place mushrooms in skillet and fry until golden brown, 1 to 2 minutes. Remove from skillet and drain on paper towel.

Artichoke hearts make a delicious substitution or addition to this recipe.

Yields: Four to six servings.

Vegetables

Woodhaven Minted Peas

⅓ c. Rhine wine
1 tsp. lemon juice
½ tsp. dried mint leaves
pinch sugar
2 tbs. butter or margarine
2 onions, peeled and diced
2 boxes frozen baby peas

In a measuring cup, combine wine, lemon juice, mint leaves and sugar. In a saucepan, melt butter or margarine, add onion and sauté until soft. Stir in wine mixture and peas, stir-frying until peas are thawed and mixture is well blended.

Cover and simmer for 3 to 4 minutes, or until everything is heated through. Turn off heat and let stand for 2 to 3 minutes before serving.

Yields: Six to eight servings.

Vegetables

Finger-Lickin' Mashed Potatoes

These mashed potatoes are *so good* that when they're finished the kitchen helpers want to lick the beaters. Save any leftovers for Must Go Omelettes.

3½ lbs. potatoes, peeled and quartered
1 pt. half 'n' half
4 tbs. butter or margarine
1 3-oz. pkg. cream cheese
¼ c. milk
2 tbs. minced onion flakes
1 tbs. mayonnaise
1 tsp. salt
⅛ tsp. freshly ground black pepper
1 tbs. grated cheddar cheese

Place potatoes in a large saucepan, cover with cold water, bring to a boil and cook for 20 minutes; drain. In a large mixing bowl, combine potatoes, half 'n' half, butter, cream cheese, milk, onion flakes, mayonnaise, salt and black pepper until smooth.

Sprinkle grated cheddar cheese over potatoes, center a large pat of butter on top and serve piping hot.

Yields: Six to eight servings.

Vegetables

Vegetables

Poppa Bear's Potato Pancakes

That's right, this recipe gets its name from the old children's story. I can't remember the number of times I've heard a firehouse cook bellow in the midst of his preparation, "Who's been eating my potato pancakes! It better stop or *else!*"

8 boiling potatoes (about 3 lbs.), peeled
2 med. onions, peeled
2 eggs
2 tsp. salt
½ tsp. cayenne pepper
¼ tsp. nutmeg
4 tbs. whole wheat flour
1 tsp. baking powder
1 c. peanut oil

Grate potatoes and onions (using grater's large hole side) directly into a colander; as quantity builds, press the mixture to squeeze out the excess liquid, then transfer to a large bowl. Repeat as necessary.

Add eggs, salt, cayenne pepper, nutmeg, flour and baking powder to mixture and mix thoroughly.

In a large, deep frying pan, heat half the oil and add a dollop of mixture (from a moderate size serving spoon) for each pancake. Then using the back of the spoon, flatten each dollop until it's approximately 3 inches in diameter. Fry over a moderate heat until crispy, golden brown on each side (approx. 4 minutes per side). Remove and drain on paper towels. Repeat until all the mixture is used.

Yields: Four to six servings.

DESSERTS

Desserts tend to be time efficient in most Big Apple firehouses. The major effort of an evening meal tends to be spent trying to "woo and wow" them with the main course. Consequently, while you will find the following desserts tasty, you'll also find their preparation simple and quick.

Desserts

Chinese Rice Dessert

1 pkg. vanilla pudding
2½ c. milk
2 c. cooked rice
½ c. raisins
2 tsp. unsweetened raspberry preserves
1 peeled apple, chopped
1 peeled banana, chopped and sprinkled with
    lemon juice
1 peeled orange, chopped

Preheat oven to 350 degrees.

Empty contents of pudding package into saucepan. Gradually add milk, stirring to keep mixture smooth. Cook over medium heat, stirring constantly, until pudding comes to a boil. Add rice, raisins and preserves.

Pour into greased round casserole dish and bake 25 minutes, or until pudding begins to bubble. Remove from heat. If dessert is to be served hot, at this point stir in chopped apple, banana and orange, and mix well. If it is to be served cold, refrigerate for 1 hour. Stir in the fruit and refrigerate for an additional hour.

Yields: Four to six servings.

Desserts

Custard from the Days of Wooden 'Plugs and Iron Firemen

2½ c. milk
4 eggs
½ c. honey
1 tsp. pure vanilla extract
½ tsp. ground cinnamon
dash salt
6 tsp. unsweetened pure raspberry preserves

Scald milk. Blend eggs with honey. Gradually stir in milk, the vanilla, cinnamon and salt into the mixture. Pour evenly into 6 custard cups, place cups in pan with hot water. Bake in preheated 350 degree oven 30 minutes, or until a toothpick inserted in center comes out clean. Serve hot or chilled topped with 1 tsp. of preserves over each serving.

Yields: Six servings.

Desserts

I Can't Be Bothered Cake

1 20-oz. can of crushed pineapple
1 can cherry pie filling
1 pkg. yellow cake mix
1 stick butter or margarine
1 c. walnuts or pecans

Preheat oven to 350 degrees.

Place fruit in a 13 × 9 baking pan. Sprinkle with cake mix straight from the box. Cut butter or margarine into pieces on top and sprinkle with nuts. Bake 1 to 1¼ hours, or until browned.

Yields: Eight to ten servings.

Firehouse Fruit Salad

8 oranges
4 tbs. honey
3 bananas
1 cut lemon
1 med. can water-packed pineapple chunks, drained
6 tsp. shredded coconut

Peel, dice, oranges; combine with honey to sweeten. Peel bananas. Cut in large pieces; squeeze with fresh lemon to keep banana from turning brown. Combine bananas and pineapple chunks with sweetened oranges. Spoon into glass serving dishes. Garnish with coconut. Serve cold.

Yields: Six servings.

Desserts

Beat That Cold Dessert

4 navel oranges, peeled, sectioned and halved
½ c. sugar
4 tbs. orange extract or Grand Marnier liqueur
3 eggs
⅓ c. heavy cream
⅛ tsp. salt

Sprinkle orange slices with ¼ c. sugar and layer them in a rectangular two-quart baking dish. Add extract or liqueur, cover and refrigerate for 2 hours. Bake oranges, covered, in preheated 350 degree oven for 20 minutes. Drain and save ½ c. juice.

Beat eggs with cream; blend in remaining ¼ c. sugar, salt and reserved juice. Pour mixture over oranges and bake, uncovered, 20-25 minutes or until custard is slightly thickened. Serve warm.

Yields: Six to eight servings.

Index

A

Antipasto, Mr. Macho's, 17
Aqueduct Chicken Escarole Soup, 14

B

Beat That Cold Dessert, 124
Beef Stew, Staten Island, 50
Belmont Barley Soup, 10
Braciole, Italian, 65
Bread, Paddy's Day, 25
Brisket, Gourmet Irish, 63
Broccoli Vita, 105

C

Cabbage, Williamsburg Stuffed, 102
Cake, I Can't Be Bothered, 123
Canarsie's Chicken Cacciatore, 78
Carrots, Castelton Corners Creamed Carrots and Cauliflower, 106
Casserole, Bensonhurst Creamy, 33
Casserole, Laurelton Reuben, 54
Casserole, SoHo Italian, 34
Cauliflower, Castelton Corners Creamed Carrots and Cauliflower, 106
Central Park Summer Lunch Salad, 16
Chili, East Village Chili on Cornbread, 56
Chinatown Chicken and Vegetables, 80
Chinese Rice Dessert, 120
Cioppino D'Amore, 94
Clams, No Holds Barred Baked, 88
Cole Slaw, Glorious Rockaway, 20

Cole Slaw, Unpretentious, 18
Crummy Chicken, 83
Custard from the Days of Wooden 'Plugs and Iron Firemen, 121

D

Dressing, Bayside Blue Cheese, 15

F

Fettucine, Rosedale's Fettucine a la Franco, 32
Firehouse Eggs, 6
Fried Fish, N'Orleans, 97
Fruit Salad, Firehouse, 123

G

Garlic Bread, Go For It, 22

H

Ham, Christmas Cherried, 69
Ham, Ridgewood's Fresh, 66
Ham Steaks, Hawaiian, 70
Hamburgers, Coney Island, 53

J

JFK Pea Soup, 12

L

Lamb Chops, Boro Park, 74
Lasagna, One-Two-Three, 38
Linguine, Whitestone's Linguine with Clam Sauce, 30
Linguini de L'Ortello, 39
Liver, Riverdale's Liver with Bacon and Mushrooms, 52
London Broil, Marinated, 58

M

Mashed Potatoes, Finger-Lickin', 115
Meat Loaf, Gramercy Park, 62
Meatballs, Firehouse Italian, 64

Mott Street Pasta e
 Fagioli, 36
Mushrooms, Midwood's
 Baked, 108
Mushrooms, Parkville
 Fried, 113
Mussels, Sheepshead
 Bay, 91

N

Noodles, Poppied, 41

O

Old MacDonald's
 Chicken, 84
Omelette, Must-go, 4
Onions, Red Devil, 111

P

Paella, Redhook, 92
Peas, G.I. Spiced, 110
Peas, Woodhaven Minted
 Peas, 114
Peppers, South Bronx
 Stuffed, 104
Popcorn, Keep 'em Up,
 24
Pork, Bowery Pork
 Tasters 'n' Kraut
 Casserole, 75
Pork Chops, Apples n',
 67

Pot Roast, Glendale, 46
Potato Pancakes, Poppa
 Bear's, 117

R

Ribs, Soul, 71
Roast Beef, Yorktown's,
 44
Roast Leg O'Lamb, Flatbush, 72

S

Salmon Cakes, Joyful, 99
Sauerbraten, Chinese, 60
Seafood New York, 98
Shirred Eggs with
 Chicken Livers, 5
Shrimp Scampi, City
 Hall, 90
Spaghetti Sauce,
 Elizabeth Street, 28
Spiced Garden Chicken,
 82
Spring Street Pasta, 40
Stroganoff, Washington
 Square, 48

T

Three-bi Eggs, 7
Tuna Salad, Sunnyside,
 19